THE WALLS BETWEEN US

e s s a y s   i n   s e a r c h   o f   t r u t h

JUNC | TURE
WRITING WORKSHOPS

CONTENTS

INTRODUCTION

We had been thinking about walls.

We had been devastated by them.

The constraining and condemning, the crooked and the crucifying. Our houses are built with walls. Our cities are. Our politics. Our moods. Our love. And, of course, our stories, with their beginnings and their ends, their particulate white spaces.

And so we invited the truth tellers among us to join us in our search to understand, delineate, and (was it possible?) shatter walls. Our call for entries was met by writers from all around the world—established and emerging and thoughtfully original writers. The stories moved and surprised us. We read them blind, attaching no names to the work until after the final round of reviews.

The Walls Between Us became a collection of sixteen full essays as well as a tapestry of voices—excerpts from pieces that seemed to speak to one another. We are graced in these pages by ferry crossings and massing birds; self-forgiveness and self-determination; motherhood, despair, grace, construction and reconstruction. Sometimes the stories are a sensory swish, and sometimes they are place-name specific. Some are funny, some are tender, some are pluck and courage. Some are noise and some are quiet. The book is its own melody. Its words come from many places, and we have maintained the authentic spellings.

We have felt nothing short of honored—reading these pages, corresponding with these writers, easing into the fonts and margins that set forth this book. We had offered prizes as part of this contest, though everyone here—indeed, everyone who wrote and shared and dared—is a winner in our eyes.

Still, in the end, it was Jillian Sullivan, with her astonishing observations of yearning, age, and mist, who took first prize. Second place was shared by Dana Schwartz, with her magnificent musing on a mother who will finally never vanish, and Fabia Oliveira, who renders a lost multicultural neighborhood with poetic heat.

We don't see walls now, when we turn the pages of this book.

We see the triumph of those who rose, and yet rise, from the bricks and mortar, the regrets and resolve.

Thank you, writers.

BETH KEPHART AND WILLIAM SULIT

THE WALLS BETWEEN US

essays in search of truth

JILLIAN SULLIVAN

Between Lands

There's a moment on the ferry crossing, mid journey, when a bird hovering over the charcoal water turns and flies towards us, wings outspread. This bird, mollymawk, suspended between waves and an apricot sky. The bird turns again, and the boat speeds on towards a bank of clouds, the plume of them covering the island, Rakiura, where tomorrow I'll be teaching.

When the ferry motored past the last ramparts of the South Island, the last rocks, I'd lifted my phone to take a photo and saw the place I'd stood seven years before, newly on my own. I'd driven to Bluff because it was the southernmost end of the South Island, the furtherest I could drive. I thought that would be a place to start, to get my bearings. And I'd stood on that ground and looked out at the ocean and wondered what would become of me. Where would I make a home? On the ferry, I salute that memory of my unknowing self. And now we're traveling beyond what I had imagined my life to be, heading full tilt into the waves toward a land of small coves, dark bush, and birds, and the ever-lapping sea, where people when they first meet you ask, "How was your crossing?"

My granddaughter Estella, who is newly three, lives on another island, Waiheke. She lives 10 hours away from me—a two-hour car trip, a two-hour wait for the plane, a two-hour flight, an hour at the airport, an hour on the bus, an hour finding my way to the ferry, an hour crossing the sea, and then the bay and the dock, the green furled hills and a small girl with curls and hesitant smile, holding her father's hand.

I want to dismiss some facts about being older. You do not stop yearning. You do not stop wanting to turn and someone is beside you. You do not stop remembering the clothesline with the tiny singlets and handmade pinafores and handwashed stripey jerseys. The small people who wore them no longer exist in any cell form on this earth, but are now six-foot-two and bearded, or have long shiny hair and a child on their lap, or are walking their dog on a beach you don't know, where there are stars out and flaxes rattling in a squiffy breeze. There are new smaller ones tucked up asleep, the books read, the apples eaten, the teeth cleaned, the water drunk, the nappies on. At home alone, I bring in an armload of wood, for stars mean frost. The curtains closed, the lamps on and the quiet of a thick-walled house saying shhhh, all is well, and it is.

The small girl, Estee, lives with her parents who are isolated too, on their island, from sisters and brothers and parents and grandparents and aunts and uncles, and from friends they once knew who knew them. And they too saying the goodnight story and passing the lidded cup of water and whispering, if not aloud, all is well. Outside, the punga ferns brush against the verandah post, the white shells glimmer on the steps, and further down the road past the fish and chip shop and the pizza cart and the swings and climbing tower, the quiet waves lift and curl like breathing onto the sand, the shells with their rounded white backs to the sky, and far away my own mountains with their white sides glistening under the moon.

On the first morning, before teaching, I walk down to the sea with my coffee. The sand is damp and flat and the sea calm. Grey like the sky. These are the quiet few moments before the hard work and the journey of the day begins. Somehow, as I walk along the beach, there needs to be a transformation, from interior dweller to leader. From going mad sinking into my own psyche to helping others sink into theirs. Gulls careen across the bay. I cross the playground and walk up the street to the library door.

In the Gulf of Mexico, there is an island called Isle de Jean Charles, and it is slowly disappearing into the sea. It is tethered to the mainland by a three-mile road, and here the sea eats and eats, until only a ragged, gravel edge remains. A child can stand there, bare feet in the water. But the school bus will no longer travel that watery highway, and on the island the hurricane-ruined houses stand empty and the sogged mattresses lie on abandoned lawns. There are grandchildren and grandparents there too, everyone almost related, but where will they go? They are standing at the bottom of the world, wondering what will become of their lives.

On Waiheke Island I wasn't sure of my direction as I drove. Estee, clipped in her carseat, watched out the window.

"There's the supermarket we went to yesterday," I said. "There's the road to your kindy. And there's the road to the beach. Shall we go swimming later?"

"Grandma, I'm a bit shy of you."

I look up at her brown eyes in the rear vision mirror.

"We don't see each other enough. I live at the bottom of New Zealand and you live at the top. Do you know baa baa black sheep?"

"Baa baa black sheep do you any wool!" We sing across the island.

One of my students, Chris, owns the restaurant on Rakiura with his wife. He said it only takes one good person in a small community and things get done. We built this hall, he said. We sawed the timbers and worked in the weekends. People did what they knew. Christchurch wants a conference centre. They're a city, and they ask—who's going to do this for us? Our hall here is the equivalent of a four-million-dollar centre. People in cities forget they can help one another, they can do things. They ask instead, who's going to do this for us?

What I want to know is, how do you hold everything in your heart? The toetoe frosted silver and snow beginning to fall in dizzy spirals, and a granddaughter's arms linked around your neck, right there beside the sea, and knowing you are it, you are Grandma.

When the class stood outside to watch the sand and the wavelets as they furled and unfurled, the temperature dropped. The rain changed from a shower that was dampening to rain that was continual and wetting. Wet jeans on thighs, the rain windblown towards the harbour, and cold legs, cold wet hands, wet notebooks. The sea and sky at one with this. I remember on an island how elemental life is. If there is a storm, you cannot leave. The island has the final say.

When I go to leave my granddaughter's island, her parents are at work. I must drive her to daycare and help her take off her sandals at the door and carry her backpack in and place it on the table. I sit on the carpet with her in a circle, while Ginny finishes reading a story about frogs. Estee's face is lifted to the story. I hope she forgets, momentarily, that when I say goodbye, I am leaving the island. I know, in a way she doesn't, that when I return she will be someone else. There'll be another story, not the frogs, and her sandals outgrown and perhaps some other favourite lunch. When I climb onto the boat it feels as if it's forever, it is like forever to a three year, two week, one day old girl. And to me.

Rakiura has steep humped sides. Even if the water rises, the island's going nowhere fast. Nor is Waiheke. That much we can be grateful for.

At the writing workshop, in our cramped room lined with books, and the long table and chairs , we write and write.

"This morning one of the guests said my fire alarm woke her," Raelene says. "I thought, fire alarm? No, it was the kiwis."

"Do they sound like this?" I ask."Kweet kweeet kweet? I heard that outside my window"

"No its more kwiiiiiiiireet kwiiireeeet."

"No like this," another said, and ended in a rumble like a man clearing his throat.

Outside rain, sun, wind, mist, rain.

Everyone has loss. Some, great loss. This is the one truth of writing groups, for this is the well we draw on for courage and humour as well as for grief. To go back and back for the strength to hold now. To hold.

We write a poem—one line each, like donating a square for a quilt to keep someone else warm. "The sea is... An island is... Choose one," I say, and I write too. There is silence, then slips of paper passed along the table.

...The sea is our borderline; it tells us where we are...

On the last morning, I teach at the local school. Thirty-two students. Not one farm on this island; the living comes from the sea. "My Dad's a fisherman," a young girl tells me. "And mine," says another. Some students come from Ireland or Christchurch or Queenstown. Some tell me "I'm eleven years old. I've lived here all my life."

There's a boy who doesn't want to write. He wants to write. He is full of story, but how to start?

"Just start," I tell him, like I tell my adult students. "It doesn't matter how you start. Something will come. You don't know what that is. You can trust it will come, though."

He grips his pen harder. It's poised over his book. Then half a minute before the timer goes off, he writes two sentences. He doesn't want to read them. When the teacher says he must, he looks to me as if I will save him.

Life will only get harder, I want to tell him. One day you'll have to go off to boarding school, you'll have to stand up, put your creative endeavours in front of those who don't know you. Better to begin here, in this small circle of islanders. Better to feel what it's like to take that leap—the fear, and then the achievement—now.

He begins to read. A small step, and I am overwhelmed again at how much courage a child needs to live. His voice is clear and measured and strong. Hearing him, one would not know the clenched pen.

"This is how it is for writers," I tell the class. "Sometimes you don't know what to say, and you have to say it."

Seven years ago when I left the North Island for the South Island, my blue car was packed to the ceiling (minus the soup pot which I'd given to my daughter). Blustery wind in Wellington. A photo shows me with my hair blown across my face. The air sharp, fresh, though it was December and summer. And all along there was a home waiting for me on the other side though I didn't know it then. A home that needed to be imagined, constructed, committed to, but it arose. I didn't know I would become strong in my arms and legs. I could have sailed from north to south and emerged as practical and capable on the other side because it was necessary, and it happened anyway. As it was, I took my positive and naive self and blundered into the building process and then grew stronger. And now I have a home, far from my children.

When I lived in Wellington there were three children out of my five living in the same city, and Estee not born. Now my children and grandchildren live in different localities, the length of New Zealand, and Australia. Is it possible we could all live near each other again? Some would have to change islands, or country, move from snow to tropical, or sea to mountains, from city to village, from mainland to island. I would have to leave my handmade house because who would choose to live in the coldest valley in the country? Here there are limited jobs and you take turns cleaning the public toilet and it's a long way to buy groceries. If we could have all chosen the same place—but we have grown idiosyncratically and have flown like particles to metal attraction. I cannot change a thing.

Yet how do you hold it all in one heart, one island?

On Isle de Jean Charles, in the southern bayous, some of the islanders want to stay, and some have already gone. What they hope for is to be together. The government has purchased a 550-acre sugarcane farm to relocate the community an hour's drive away.

"What are they going to do when they get there?" asks 81-year-old Theo Chaisson, interviewed for the *Independent*. These are islanders who have always made their living from the sea. "You think they'll have oysters in their backyard, speckled trout, red fish, shrimp? No." Yet they'll be joined again by pathways, from grandparent to grandchild, friend to friend.

The binds of a land lived in for seven generations hold strong. Though this land was once a forest of oak and fir, and now smells of the rot of salt-infused trees, there are those who don't want to go. "I'll tell them, 'No, no, no'," says Chaisson. Maybe only his grandchildren will grow up amongst the scent of sugarcane.

We are a turbulent world, one criss-crossed by those who leave, those who search for a new home, hearts wracked by memories of those they leave behind, and their land, but also by the daily living with such loss. To be disunited.

I walk away from my granddaughter to the car, then to the ferry. I stand on the aft deck for the crossing, facing the sea, arms crossed over my stomach for balance. I watch the waves churn and the island recede, bearing witness to the distance lengthening between us. One small bay becomes an island, becomes a dark horizon, becomes one island among headlands and other islands, becomes diminutive in the expanse of sea and sky. Behind me the obelisks of the city rise.

How do we live without the people we love? It is a question that has no simple answer or solution. We are condemned to loneliness. We leave or are left by the small ones, or the old ones, or our own ones. The landscape changes inexorably: rivers we once swam in now cannot be entered, trees we once loved have been felled. There were open spaces we once gazed across, now blocked by fences, by malls. We live with this, too.

I place my suitcase on the asphalt at the city end. People brush past me. I don't know how to carry on. How to walk my way to the bus. Back to my life of mountain, valley, tussock, hawk.

On Rakiura, before I left, the sea was grey, the surface roughened by wind. A low surge of water rolled over itself into foam. The boats faced the shore. Their ropes leading to matching orange buoys looped in that space between air and water. The boats, lightly held on the surface of the sea.

DANA SCHWARTZ

———

The Walls Within

In my dreams, the structure is unsound. Scaffolding ensnares the house, workers scale the walls, and milk rivulets down pregnant ceilings.

For a year after my mother's death, I had recurring nightmares about my childhood home. Strangers and wild animals roamed the surrounding woods and crouched inside my closet. Storms raged outside, and wild parties within. Ceilings bowed under the weight of mysterious liquids.

Once there was a fire and it was my fault. I ran through the smoke-filled rooms trying to save what I could. The cats, my mother's art. Outside I watched helplessly as my father's silhouette moved behind the upstairs windows. Then I blinked, and the windows were boarded up, the house was a burnt-out shell. Somehow the fire was happening and had already happened.

For years I assumed these dreams were a result of grief. My subconscious was deconstructing the past by laying siege on a core memory. I was the passive bystander, night after night, whether I was running toward the house or away from it.

Eventually the dreams about my house stopped, as did the ones about my mother. Despite my desire for their return, they drifted away as time went on. I wanted to keep my grief close; pain was my connection. Without grief's incessant pulse and throb, my mother's vitality began to dull, like the shine of autumn leaves that fade to brown and crumble under careless or deliberate feet.

*

My mother and I were close.

She was a good mother.

I was a good daughter.

This is the story I told myself, what others told me. After she died I began to question my role, wondering what was true and what was façade. Like all organic material, the walls of our relationship began to break down. Surrounded by the wreckage, I started to dig, unearth, examine. I kept circling back to my childhood home. In my dreams first, and then in my examination of them.

What does it mean when a home, so lovingly built, so carefully tended, comes under siege?

The house was built on top of a staggering hill, and for a while, it seemed like a refuge, a safe place to perch. Floor-to-ceiling windows flanked the front door, gazing down at the neighborhood below like giant unblinking eyes. This mirrored exterior proved problematic for the birds, who zoomed toward the reflected branches at high speed only to smash into the glass and drop like stones on the deck below. Our cat disposed with the corpses if we didn't find them first.

My parents moved out of the house a few weeks before my mother's rapid decline. A domino effect, perhaps triggered by the move, but her failing health was a much longer and winding road, traveling back almost two decades with her diagnosis of multiple sclerosis at age forty. MS is an autoimmune disease where the body attacks itself, specifically the protective sheath around the nerves called myelin. Walls are breached; lines are cut. Messages never reach their destination. Imagine a body filled with broken wires.

Though her first visible symptom was her shuffling, clumsy gait, my

mother soon lost the use of her hands. Hands that were once nimble and strong. Hands that pounded clay, molding and shaping it into bowls, platters, vases, and masks. Hands that had comforted and caressed lost their agility. Forks clattered to the ground, embraces weakened.

Our lives changed, her life changed—rapidly, ruthlessly.

Within a handful of years, she lost the ability to walk and feed herself. My father filled the void, bought gadgets, hired help. We tried to maintain the shape of our lives from before. *Nothing has to change*, my father used to say, his way of preserving order in chaos, but of course everything did.

We bowed beneath the weight of it all, but we also adapted. Life went on as scheduled, for us, while my mother learned to live within her new, broken body. Often this meant being left behind, literally, in the house. What did she think about when she was alone? How did she feel about her art displayed in acrylic cubes on the walls, the clear panes gathering dust? The masks within gazing back at her with their anguished expressions, some mirroring hers since she used her face as a mold. Was it a painful reminder, or an anchor to the past?

I don't know. I never asked.

After my mother's death the house remained filled, but empty. She was our constant, the sun around which we orbited, and when she died, everything went dark. The ground beneath us lost its solidity, the walls shook.

*

We all begin in the same place, the same house. Within the walls of our mother, in her uterus. Safe and protected, we are not alone. Shortly after conception, the placenta begins to form. This new and temporary organ is unique because it's made from embryonic cells and the mother's uterine tissue. It belongs to us both.

During pregnancy, cells from mother to baby travel back and forth through the placenta. They intermingle, cross borders. This phenomenon is called microchimerism, originating from the word, *chimera*, the Greek fire-breathing monster with the head of a lion, the body of a goat, and the tail of a serpent. Mother and baby carry each other's cells within their bodies during—and after—birth.

I find this comforting, and it's something I understood intuitively even before I learned about the scientific explanation—that my mother will always be part of me. What I didn't know is that we also leave something behind. Fetal cells have been found in healed Cesarean-section scars as well as in healthy organs, indicating a possible role in disease prevention. But higher levels of fetal cells also have been linked to autoimmune illnesses such as scleroderma and multiple sclerosis.

Though this research is new and preliminary, it was jarring to consider the possibility that my cells might have played a role in my mother's illness, her terrible fate. Much has been said and written about the myriad of ways parents scar their children, but what about the other way around? I suppose it only makes sense. None of us can walk through life without harming others, no matter our best intentions. We all leave a mark, and in some cases, our cells.

I think my mother would have become pregnant even if she had known about this risk, however theoretical, however slight. She would have taken her chances, rolled the dice. Motherhood was one of her greatest accomplishments, she used to say, which was a gift to me as a daughter, but a burden when I became a mother. Could I live up to her example? Did I want to?

*

Less than a year after my mother's death, I had a baby, a little girl. Not long after, my father put our family house on the market. It took almost two years to sell. Days before the closing, I visited one final time, bringing my toddler daughter. She raced through the empty rooms with glee, skidding across the hardwood floors in her socks until we pried them off. It reminded me of when I was four and my father brought me alone to the newly razed plot of land, the site of our future home.

Memories of this day have multiplied in my mind like an infinity mirror, the original overlapping with the dozens of times I viewed the grainy video footage. There I am, at the top of the hill, the crisp autumn wind swirling my hair. I'm surveying the white chalk outline on the freshly turned earth while my father narrates from behind the camera in a low and distorted voice.

"It's November 1979. Dana is walking through front entrance of our house."

After a few moments, I stop following his cues and begin to run, my canvas purse slapping against my side, my hair rippling like a flag. I trip over a root sticking out of the ground but quickly get up, flashing a smile at my father.

"There she is," he says, as I pause to catch my breath, "about to jump out the window!"

Grinning, I leap over the chalked line.

Thirty years later, while saying goodbye to the house, I told my husband to take a picture of me nursing our daughter on the couch, in the same spot I used to sit beside my mother. I wished she could be in the frame with us, but now I take comfort in knowing she was.

*

The house belongs to another family now, imprinting their memories into rooms whose geography I will never forget. It has taken years, but I know why the foundation was cracking in my dreams. It wasn't grief shaking the walls, but me. I was testing their strength, pushing against them. I needed to see what would hold and what would fall.

In those early weeks of searing pain, it was impossible to understand what over time has become so simple and clear. Certain walls can't break, they won't crumble.

You carry them with you.

FABIA OLIVEIRA

———

A Blue Wall

Our backyard, the cherished living space for children lucky enough to have such a thing, was a parking lot. From all over the world our families had come to reside here in a squat, red building on a main avenue of a hilly city named Somerville. All around us old Victorian fortresses had been raised up, some now sinking into their foundations. They had grass and they had yews with berries; shouldn't the blue jays have gathered there? What did they want with our pavement and weather-worn fence? Why, under tired branches of this sullen, singular oak, did that massing happen?

With determination, is how I would describe our afternoons of play. The serious work of children was ours for the next few years at most. Together we mapped out an understanding of this blue-collar life. Some of us had single moms. Some of us had single moms and half siblings. Some, like me, had two parents and two cultures living side by side, strangers in an experiment called the nuclear family.

It seemed to me that we were all trying to rattle the fences, pull down the building that cooped us up, brick by brick, year by year, with earnest fingers and words.

"You're too fat," one would say.

"You're too dark." Another.

"You're not that smart," came more infractions.

There must have been reasons why we lived the way we did. Not poor, not homeless, but never, no never good enough. Just making it. Some with stamps approving them for food. Others with mops and sprays put to work on someone else's marble counters and hardwood floors. Not like our wall-to-wall carpeted one-and two-bedroom worlds. We expanded our living spaces by sharing our corners. A playdate in the neighbor's bedroom provided a view of the dry cleaner's parking lot, tufts of weeds at the edges fighting a war with the cement. Another apartment, up carpeted steps, looked out at the skyline over the tops of pitched roofs, though, by dusk, the shadows lay too slant for dreams.

A camaraderie of misfits. A sense of belonging in a world the likes of which we may never find again. We stuck to one another, different as wildflowers, for safety. Things happened that we did not yet understand. Things in our bodies that we couldn't name. Once, a flashing of budding breasts to a friend. Another time, walking home in the shame of wet jeans, too old to piss ourselves, too young to know that trauma was to blame. We used crude language to describe the mysteries of what lay ahead. We were bored by the continuation of childhood. We felt challenged by the cars that sped past us going somewhere on our main avenue, for we were stuck, trying like the weeds to grow out of the concrete.

The cadences of our lives held foreboding. We wondered about the shack that stood beside our red brick turf, abandoned. Inside those collapsing walls were buckets of fossilized paint and a dead sea of brown clutter. How were we to make a life from that? We were looking for clues about our future, watching the adults who governed our world. Did we see, in what was broken, the work that needed to be done within ourselves? Did we draw on our rented walls places only we could see?

"We don't own this place, you can't do that!"

When, I wanted to ask, would I be allowed to make my realm grander? And with what tools? Crayons are children's tools. They had no place in a grown-up existence. That's what I was learning. Around me were house cleaners, cooks, homemakers. What did they know about a crayon's utility?

On the day the birds came we had lost ourselves to a travel through time. We had chosen our steps carefully among the tangled vines of a prehistoric forest. We were alert to the sounds of the gargantuan beasts we would have to tame. Struggles lay ahead—a time of chaos, a loss of identity in a forest thicker than the ones we were pretending to traverse. With mock swings, I had cut down vines, the machete weighing on me. How else would we be safe in the jumble of imaginary green?

At first I thought we had really succeeded in make-believe, like when I had once been convinced of making headway digging to China. Like when, in the home of a babysitter who barely looked at me, I chanted with the children on TV "I believe, I believe" and waited for the plush toy in my lap to grow, with a twinkle in his eye, into a life-sized dinosaur, a friend.

But now, above our heads, was the sound of caws, gaining momentum.

"Look! A blue jay!"

A rarity. And now, down by our sneakered feet, the jungle was disappearing as if in a mist. What was left in its place was a cracked, charcoal pavement, black and devoid of give, and on it lay a small blue body void of flight. One wing spread away from its downturned face, like how I slept at night.

"Don't touch it!"

We had been warned of germs. But about the business of dying, we knew practically nothing. Round and round we circled the bird, squatting and then standing, our shadows covering its parts. Such a foreign thing, this stillness before us. Our own muscles seemed to pulse in a constant, unwanted frenzy.

The dainty feet of the blue jays now clung to our fence. Were there hundreds of them? Twenty? Something was amiss. Their calls grew louder. We sat now, ankles crossed as if in prayer, on the cold ground near the bird. We looked up and finally the sensible walls of all we had been told to expect gave way to the illusory world we knew in our ancient hearts existed. There, above us, the blue wall of birds was talking. The birds were summoning friends and loved ones. The birds were a chorus of mourning.

JESSICA GILKISON

————

(Wall)...As Protection...As Barrier...As Boundary

The first time she kicked a hole in the wall of her suburban ranch she kept it a secret for months. She had slammed her bedroom door, pivoted left, and pushed her right foot through layers of paint, drywall, and plaster in mere seconds. She covered it with a decorative hanging, but the odd placement just a couple feet off the ground caught her mother's eye. Her parents were angry, but at some point her dad patched the hole. He knew how to do stuff, but if you squatted and leaned in close you could tell there'd been a repair where the edges of the fix bled into the original wall.

*

What walls her mind created to keep the darkness at bay. She was a child construction worker given no instructions on how to lay brick, to slather the mortar, to stack and pile until a sufficient barrier was in place.

She never consented to your entrance of room or body. Is alcohol an excuse? Is 'I'm sorry' enough? Is 'I don't remember' a cop-out? How hard did you have to work to forget? She labored nights building her self-protection, no minimum wage, no overtime. Do you really not remember or is that the fiction you feed yourself in order to survive? She has no such luxury.

She read *The Secret Garden* and *The Lion, the Witch, and the Wardrobe*, fascinated by barriers that could protect something sacred or transport you to another world. She was drawn to the space between herself and the truth, between herself and you, but the back of her wardrobe led nowhere. She studied how other children handled danger. You bred shame in her bones, but she learned to pretend her shrubs were untrampled and the rose bushes pristine. She knew something was wrong. She knew, until she helped herself forget and silence settled in. The forgetting unraveled when she left home. Remembering happens in an instant but that instant can take years to unfold.

Did you know your brain could create a tiny room for the terrible things that happened to you as a child, where you can slam the door shut and live without conscious knowledge? But the wood on the door to that room starts to rot and the hinges grow loose. The cobwebs that accumulate over all those years brush against your lips and get caught in your eyelashes when you crack the door open and peek inside. You reach in and flick the light switch, but the bulb is dead or the electricity isn't on. Don't worry, though. You'll be able to see everything inside soon enough.

*

The second time she kicked a hole in the wall she was not able to hide it. Maybe this time she didn't want to, or perhaps she simply could not contain her rage until she reached her bedroom at the end of the hall. Maybe she wanted this hole to be seen, to say *hey, we cannot pretend any longer*, to force her parents to see evidence of her pain. But this time her dad didn't patch it up. Instead, her parents decided she would need to learn how to repair the damage she had caused.

Her dad handed her a Time Life book from the 'Fix-It-Yourself' series. She avoided the task as long as possible, like all household chores. "This pan needs to soak overnight," was the phrase she uttered most frequently during adolescence. When she could not avoid it any longer, she gathered the supplies—some sort of mesh patch she cut to slightly larger than the hole, a tub of spackle spread to cover in a crisscross, feathered pattern; then allow to dry, sand, and paint.

Neither hole was large enough for the truth to fit through. Her foot had breached the wall in the shape of her rage. She was held accountable, to a higher standard than he was.

He respected the U.S. Mail, would never open something addressed to another person, even junk mail. He respected the privacy of journals and other papers. Yet somehow he had not respected the privacy of her body.

Now she spends her spare time removing bricks one by one to let the light in.

BETH ANDERSON

———

Hunt for the Wild Kiwi

"You can live your whole life in New Zealand and never see a Kiwi," the locals told me. Thus my obsession began.

My husband, son, and daughter had agreed to come with me on a never-ending bus ride switchbacking through the rainforests of Northern New Zealand in search of the Kiwi , the Holy Grail of the Pacific Islands. The three of them sat on the bench at the last bus stop, my husband with a map, my son staring off, no doubt thinking of ways to get even with me, my daughter making small piles of New Zealand coins on her thighs, counting out enough fare for us to get on yet another bus to get to the rescued pair of Kiwis that I realized at this late hour were only rumored to be at the rural museum.

After a short while on the third bus the driver finally said, "At the end of the line, folks."

My kids looked at me and I confidently led my family off the bus, the empty parking lot boding ill.

"Look at that. It's still open," my son said.

Oh, thank God, I thought. I had no Plan B.

We filed into a small, white office, apparently the only visitors. "Hallooo! Come in, come in," a cheery voice greeted us. "Where are you from?" asked a woman in a workshirt and brand spanking new Levis. Grey hair spiraled around her head. "Lila," her name tag read.

"Seattle," my husband said.

Lila jumped up from her chair and with her hand over her heart she proclaimed in an excited British voice that only excited British people can do, "I want to come to America and go to Vashon Island."

We all took a step back from this exuberant display of enthusiasm.

"My favorite author of all time is Betty MacDonald from Vashon Island, America. I want to see this magical place she wrote about."

Really? Vashon Island? That common bump of a place I looked at every damn day as a kid? Lila said this with such passion and reverence that I felt silly for not knowing who she was talking about.

Lila came out of her homage moment to Betty whoever and said, "So I assume you are here to see our new couple." Enormous smile, lots of English teeth.

"In fact, we have traveled all day to see them," my husband said.

"That is fantastic!" She turned to the grainy screen over her shoulder. A form that looked like a 1980s ultrasound breathed in a dark huddle. "There they are. Our precious birds. Only arrived Friday so they are still too shy to come out of their box." She beamed at the screen.

"Um. Are we able to see them?" my son asked.

"Of course. Do you see the beak just there?" She pointed at a sliver of light.

My son looked at me. It's always my fault, you see.

"You can go take a look in their enclosure through there." Lila waved an arm to a plain, white door. "You must be silent. They are still adjusting."

The kids and I filed through the door only to be in a hallway which led to another door. Top security, these birds. There were a few tanks with other rare creatures in them. Again, thank God. My son knelt down to look directly at a Giant Tuatara, a rare, endangered lizard which looked just like the one by the pool the previous day. It sat frozen on a rock in all its endangeredness, soaking up the rays from the light bulb above it.

I went first through the door to the enclosure. It seemed we were in total darkness until our eyes adjusted and could make out a huge glass enclosure. We walked around it to a faint light emitting from a wooden box, obviously the one housing the elusive pair.

We watched, holding our breath.

"It's just a box," my daughter whispered and left through the next door.

My son and I stared at the box. We stared at that box until I was seeing imprints on my retinas. Footsteps quickly rushed back into the room. My daughter.

"One is coming out!" she hissed.

I opened my eyes wider so as not to miss it. A bit of rustling, then the tip of a beak, then more beak. Finally a whole curved, skinny beak and a reflection of a round, black eye.

I urged that bird to come out with my best human-to-bird telepathic abilities. My whole reputation as the leader of this family outing, and any future ones, was at stake. To no avail. The eye disappeared and the beak slowly retreated into the darkness of that damn box.

Resigned to defeat, I followed my son out to the brightness of the office where Lila gushed to my husband as they watched the screen.

"I feel so honored to be allowed to work with these magnificent creatures." Her eyes welled with tears. My husband nodded in agreement with her. "I wish you could see them properly. But it's not like I can go in there and poke them with a stick, now can I?"

Well, you could, I thought.

The museum closed and we waited in the parking lot in the oncoming dusk. A few raindrops pelted my face. I prayed the bus would return as promised. Some kind of giant mechanical vehicle barrelled past on the left side of the foreign road.

I paced, not wanting to hear the complaints of this all-day venture to see a beak, and we still weren't guaranteed to make it back. I finally sat on the arm of the bench with my family ready to take it on the chin.

"That was one of the coolest things I've ever seen," said my son.

"Right?" said my daughter.

My husband looked at Lila's business card with her handwritten email, smiled, and tucked it into his wallet.

SHERRY SHAHAN

———

The Boat

It must've been the summer of 1957, which would've put me between the third and fourth grade.

Tony and Anita Bierbaumer, which sounded like Beer Bomber to me, lived a few blocks from our house in Canoga Park. Anita and my mom were best friends, though their connection is lost to history.

Tony owned a filling station, the kind where a squeaky clean guy in a button-down, collared shirt pumped gas, washed windshields, checked tire pressure. No extra charge. He'd change your oil and charge your battery. All cash. Bankcards were still a novelty. In 1959, American Express launched the first 'plastic' card. Previous cards were cardboard or celluloid.

Gas hovered at 19-cents a gallon. Fill 'er up for less than four bucks. Earnings from the filling station provided the Bierbaumers with a Chris-Craft cabin cruiser. I saw it whenever the garage door was up. Man, only movie stars and presidents had boats like this.

A swimming pool took up half their backyard, shaped like a big blue, watery kidney bean. Oil-fueled tiki torches wavered outside a tiki hut where we changed into our swimsuits.

Twin sons Larry and Gary were marginalized, developmentally slow from lack of oxygen in the birth canal. The six-foot tall fifteen-year-olds didn't have any friends in the neighborhood. I didn't have many friends either. We became a little allied nation by default.

I have to interrupt at this point to relate the twin's secret tale—probably heard from their older brother, whose face and name have been sucked from my cerebrum—of prostitutes having sex with donkeys on barroom stages in a country called Tijuana. They laughed like crazy, and I laughed too, loved being in on the joke, though I didn't know what they were talking about.

The twins taught me armpit farts, which I used to torture my younger brother. I taught them how to blow bubbles off the tip their tongues. Tiny spit bubbles could float forever.

Since I don't remember the name of their older brother let's call him Dick. He was a year or two older than the twins and clean cut, could've been his own twin to Eddie Haskell on *Leave it To Beaver*. You know the sickening type, always sucking up to adults.

Behind his parents' backs Dick tortured his brothers until they wet themselves. The smart thing would've been to stay on his good side, but I hated him too much to lick his penny loafers.

Anyhow, back to my mom and Anita and their glamorous girlfriends. Audrey had the same cat-green eyes as Elizabeth Taylor. Her husband owned the largest western nightclub east of the Mississippi. Orchid had a flamboyant mass of red hair accentuated with a fall—a popular kind of a hair-piece wiglet. Her muscled, freckle-faced husband was a city cop. On duty, he'd stand on the deck of the pool in his uniform, instructing us in cannonballs off the diving board.

Every one of these women struck movie star poses poolside, parading in gauzy cover-ups, hair swept into sleek waves, accentuating rhinestone clip-on earrings. A tall, frosty glass with a sprig of mint or orange slice finished off their ensembles. They were so *Vogue*.

I was bonkers over their backless pastel pumps with pom-pom flowers. Not one of them perspired. Not ever. I have volumes of fifty-year-old photo albums to prove it. Fake leather covers, four-inch thick plastic sheets protecting their perfect figures.

On Mom's day off she'd lounge in the Bierbaumers' backyard in the shade of a woven aluminum umbrella. Unlike me, Daddy, and my brother, my mom never touched water. Not wading in the ocean or dangling her feet in a pool. I used to think it was because she didn't want to mess up her hair or makeup. But now I think she was afraid of anything that moved.

My brother Steve sat on the steps in the shallow end. His inflatable water wings endowed him with neon-green biceps. My dirty-blonde hair turned the same weird color, floating around my face while I had an underwater tea party.

I don't recall if the Bierbaumers were Daddy's pool-cleaning clients. Maybe that's how they met? Or, maybe it was at the filling station, swapping dirty jokes, matching each other beer for beer? Some things are blurry.

But I have a clear memory of one afternoon, diving in the pool with the twins, collecting pennies and nickels off the bottom—and of coming up for air and seeing Dick spying on me from inside the living room. He stood by the sliding glass doors, partially hidden by shimmery drapes. The water from the pool splashing onto the sizzling hot concrete deck was about to be seared off.

Dick opened the slider, nodding his blockhead. *Pssst!*

I had that fizzy feeling. "Has anyone ever told you how cute you are?"

I expected him to say something about my freckles like everyone else.

"And sexy." Then he dangled an irresistible carrot. "Want to see the inside of the boat?"

And, so I nibbled the bait.

I tagged behind him to the garage where he flipped on the overhead light, and took a folding ladder from a peg on the wall, hooking it over the stern. "Stay clear of the propellers," he said and offered a hand. "You first."

Once inside the cabin, he took me on a tour, pointing out the fake-wood-paneled head with a toilet that really flushed, and the galley with its playhouse size stove and fridge. My doll Betsy Wetsy would've love it. And, finally, the berths. The beds had comfy-looking red-and-green plaid spreads.

"My brothers bunk here when we go to Catalina."

I let him boost me up, bouncing on the foam mattress, having so much fun I forgot who I was with until he told me to take off the bottom of my swimsuit. I must've looked like I didn't hear him, because he repeated it. "If you don't, I'll beat the twins bloody."

I imagined the pool filled with a glob of guts.

So I did it; I took off my suit. The bedspread made my butt itch.

He grabbed and grabbed before wiggling out of his trunks and holding out a nubbin of a penis. (I'd seen my brother's plenty of times in the bathtub. But this one had hair. So *dumb*.) Pressing his hands against my shoulders, he held me down and positioned his puny penis between my legs.

I don't remember any pain. But I was unable to say *no* or *stop* because I wasn't even there. I knew how to be invisible. Sometimes invisible felt like an actual place.

A few thrusts with his bony hips and a pathetic grunt.

Dick beamed, proud of himself. "Better keep your mouth shut, if you know what's good for you."

I had no interest in telling anyone what had happened. I didn't cry, or even sniffle, struggling to put my swimsuit on, wishing it could shield me. I saw my chance to get away when he left.

I climbed out of the boat and walked in the house through the living room passing a monster TV in a cabinet with a hi-fi—to the swimming pool, where Larry and Gary were in a splash war in the deep end.

During that time I became obsessed with the biology of baby-making. I pestered Mom constantly. "Honey, we just talked about that," she'd say. "Don't you remember?"

A straight-faced lie: "I forgot—tell me again." And she did.

Never mind that I wouldn't get my period for another seven years; I believed slimy Dick seeds were growing inside me. The slightest bellyache turned into morning sickness, as did the stomach flu. I threw up imagining baby seeds drowning in the toilet. But . . . what if some stuck to my ribcage?

I borrowed the tape measure from my grandmother's sewing kit and wrapped the yellow paper around my waist. Day in, day out, I tallied the black lines, recording quarter inches in code. This went on for years.

When people talked about having babies I had no flipping sense what that meant. I certainly didn't imagine that a living, breathing creature would emerge from the same place I peed.

Mom didn't include this in her tutorial, and while I vaguely remember her watermelon belly when pregnant with my brother, I couldn't conceptualize it. I never considered how the little guy got out of there.

On one of those breathless summer days, Mom and Anita rounded up us kids for a beach outing. My brother, Steve, and me, twins Larry and Gary, and Dick. Seven of us squeezed into a four-door sedan, cramped and cranky, sticking to the ribbed vinyl seats. No air conditioner. No seatbelts, which weren't invented for another two years.

I was pinned next to Dick, his sweat-soaked body crushing me against the door handle. And, I was suddenly terrified I'd have to marry him, because only married people had babies. And equally terrifying: I'd be having a baby before I'd memorized my multiplication tables.

Mom and Anita bubbled up, singing off-key to The Everly Brothers, "All I have to do is Dream."

Soon after turning onto PCH I saw a tractor-trailer through a smudge in the side-view mirror. It filled the lane directly behind us, piled high with new cars, and was picking up speed.

Then Anita noticed it in her mirrors. "Oh, my gawd!"

Dick squealed like a pig and crouched in an oddly similar way to the position he'd taken over me on the boat. His skinny neck flushed the same crimson, only now he cried like a big fat baby. "Don't let me die! I don't want to die!"

God, it was magnificent seeing him grovel like this in front of all of us. The twins pointed and laughed loudly, clearly as unconcerned as I was about being crushed by tons of steel. Then, we were still, while Dick tried to fold into the space between the front and back seats, clasping his hands and pleading with the heavens. "Please Jesus, please don't let me die!"

Not us, but me.

The truck must've found its brakes because it swerved around us and we were saved. But I didn't care about that, and I don't think the twins did either, because Dick no longer had power over us. He knew it, too. I could tell.

KRISTINA MORICONI

(Re)Construction

Suppose I told you this story is mostly about sadness. There are bones and birds, but really it is about my missing a man who built train cars and dollhouses and stone walls. A man who shot jackrabbits and armadillos and traded them for cigarettes during the war. A man who read Louis L'Amour westerns. Who jiggled pocket change. Who let me sip Sambuca when I was twelve.

What I write begins as an *excavation*, a systematic digging, recording. A want to know more.

Analysis: The process of studying and classifying artifacts.

Artifact: Any object made, modified, or used by people.

You see where I'm going with this. Working from the known to the unknown. From the top to the bottom.

*

I move into in the house on the corner where I once stood, decades before, waiting for the school bus.

My first spring in this house, in the garden, I wait as green pushes its way through the soil. Grow, I whisper, bloom. I want to know everything that remains, what is hidden, what has been left behind.

The family of six who lived here before had moved out in a hurry.

Already, I've unearthed a wedding gown in the basement, yards of white satin and lace balled up on the dirty wet floor.

Outside, tightly wrapped buds fringe the branches of winter's brown. I anticipate the shock of color, each surprise, each shade unveiling itself as part of a larger plan.

What ended suddenly here will soon be eclipsed by the story of what carries on. Roots will take hold, keep new soil from washing away.

I dig holes deep in the freshly tilled earth, plant Juniper and Chokeberry, Hibiscus and Big Blue. Along the new fence, I pile artifacts exhumed from the ground, objects from another life, small bits of a family, now extinct:

Four baseballs I imagine being thrown by a father before he left, before weather frayed the seams, exposing layers of string wound around a cork center underneath.

Three disembodied plastic arms of action figures. Somewhere, Iron Man, Hulk, Captain America abandoned, each without an arm. And perhaps a boy who has tossed what remains of his heroes into a toy box, never to play with them again.

Two glass marbles: crystal blue Cat's Eyes.

One plastic egg, still waiting to be found, hidden once by a mother or a father in a crumbling stone wall, before something cracked it open, took what had been tucked inside.

*

Context: The relationship of artifacts and other cultural remains to each other and the situation in which they are found.

A crumbling stone wall is a *context.*

*

Along the sloped garden in the backyard of this house, part of the wall has collapsed. Other parts are beginning to buckle and give way. What had been there is covered in moss and lichen, entire worlds of green: root structures, leaves, stems. Rosette patterns spreading across rocks of schist.

I will shore it up, rebuild it, try not to disturb what is already there. But, as I lift rocks, move them around, mice and chipmunks scatter. Hawks swoop down, snatch them from the grass.

As I stack one rock on top of another, stagger and restructure, I am reminded of childhood days spent leaping from the wall in my grandparents' backyard, a wall my grandfather built with stones he'd selected and hauled straight from the quarry near his house. A self-taught stonemason.

*

I collect data, interpret, try to reconstruct a life out of memory and stone. I suppose there is sadness in this process, this reconstruction.

Perhaps this is my only truth.

Consider how abstract truth can seem, until you find something tangible to hold onto.

*

In dry stone wall construction, *foundation* stones are the largest in the wall and may be partly or entirely below ground. *Through* stones extend from one side to the other, connecting the two faces. The top stones are called the *cope*.

*

As a child, the wall in my grandparents' backyard seems like a high perilous ledge, one I jump from to challenge my fears, to dare myself to fly, to land farther and farther each time.

With my cousins, in elaborate games of survival and search and rescue, we hide things behind the loose rocks in the wall. We hide notes and coins and pocket knives. We hide slingshots, stockpile small rocks as ammunition. We hide marbles and matchbooks, the body of a dead bird we find in the backyard.

This bird becomes our secret. We watch, with odd fascination, the time-lapse of its decay.

Small pieces of grit in its gut. The neck snapped, its head resting on a few splayed feathers left on one wing. Its mandible hinged open, some-thing hooked in the throat, something else in the V-shaped breach of its beak.

One black-onyx eye remains, the other already plucked from its orbital ring. Before this bird becomes ours to study. Its keeled sternum, cracked wishbone, its crooked feet.

Excavation involves the recovery of several different types of data from a site.

A decomposing bird is an *ecofact*.

*

I suppose there is sadness in this process, this decomposition. But we look at it with wonder. With childhood curiosity.

The same way we look at the canned goods stacked on the shelves of our grandparents' pantry in their basement. Hundreds of cans of vegetables and fruit, as though there might be a dire shortage of food any day.

The same way we sneak into the heater room, too, to stare at the skins of rattlesnakes our grandfather keeps there, hanging on the walls.

The same way we hide behind the bar our grandfather built studying his collection of vintage liquor bottles. Empty, sticky bottles shaped like pirates and soldiers, birds and sexy women in bikinis. These, he tells us, had come from his years down south driving trucks filled with alcohol and tobacco.

This assemblage. These artifacts found together. *In situ:* in the original place.

*

Years later, I visit my grandparents' house with my own children. Holding onto my hand, they walk along the stone wall. They are too young to jump, but I tell them my stories of flying.

The wall seems so much lower to me now, so much less intimidating.

One Sunday, I stop by on my way to Sears to have my daughters' first professional pictures taken. My grandfather is in the kitchen. Not long after we arrive, he begins coughing. Fast, it becomes uncontrollable, almost choking, until blood rushes from his mouth out onto the floor, drips down onto his white t-shirt.

I freeze for a few seconds. Then I remember my daughters are seeing this. I hurry them into another room with my grandmother before returning to the kitchen. My grandfather stands at the sink, still coughing up blood, so red against the white porcelain.

I call 9-1-1.

I know then I will write about this someday. About the bright red of his blood. About his lungs and how they are filled with cancer. About how, because he smoked cigarettes for years, the diagnosis of asbestosis is complicated. Inconclusive.

But I know.

Consider how uncertain knowing can seem, until you find something tangible to hold onto.

Proof. Evidence. In those train cars he helped to build, asbestos insulated almost everything. He'd handled it. Inhaled it. And the fibers had penetrated deep into his lungs.

Later that day, my daughters still in their fancy dresses, I take them to Sears to have their picture taken. They both smile.

A photograph is a *context*. It will always remind me. I know.

*

I am there when he takes his last breath. In those final moments, he pleads with me to finish roofing and painting and decorating the dollhouse he built for me years before, the one sitting near his workbench in the basement. He apologizes for not finishing it, but he wants me to pass it on to my own daughters.

An unfinished dollhouse is a *use-related context*, resulting from abandonment of materials during its construction.

*

As I rebuild the wall in my backyard, I hear the sound of my grandfather's voice: *One stone over two, two stones over one.*

In between the *face* stones, I tuck the *hearting*, small stones that fill in the gaps, that make the wall structurally sound. I heart the wall tightly as I go.

I miss the man who taught me. Who would point to the wall he'd built in his backyard and name the stones. Who'd show me the layers of mica and graphite in the sparkling rocks of *schist*.

Schist, from the Greek, meaning "to split."

*

I till the soil around this new wall, plan a new garden. The earth, loosened, yields a skeleton key, a small plastic hand, shards of a blue and white Spode plate.

And, just a few feet away, the body of a bird, lifeless. Fresh. Its feathers still untouched.

The only damage so far, the hollowed socket of one eye.

I study the pattern of color. A purple finch resting in my cupped palm.

We are burial places, Leonardo da Vinci writes.

Suppose I told you this is the exact moment I begin piecing together my own words, feeling the weight of sadness, spinning this into story. All of it.

Because there is no escaping this life.

You see how I'd been captivated early on by the shiny surfaces of plastic bits, their bright colors. By the taint of time on baseballs and birds. By the comforting smell of earth and everything, once buried, it is willing to relinquish.

How I want—no, need—to collect and chronicle these remnants of the past, tell the story of how they reveal themselves. How they resurrect the dead.

VICTORIA PUNCH

————

Will I Ever

It started slowly. Like the turn of the tide, or a winter's dusk. The edges of my world were being rubbed out, my peripheral vision eroded. Less like a fog rolling in, and more like a mist rising. When the threshold of perception was reached, it was already too late.

Sometimes the strangest things happen, unexplained by science, a mystery underneath the medical jargon and tests. Sometimes a long dark tunnel is actually a chrysalis; the means of transformation that is not possible in a day-lit, open-skied life.

That buried, underground experience, the scratching and stripping back, the breaking down of the body's balances, can lead to a reimagining of what life could be.

*

I always hated running. At school, high up in the hills of Kenya, compulsory early-morning cross-country training took us through a long eucalyptus forest, the dirt red on our gym socks.

The trees were beautiful. Lined up far off as we started out, bleary and grumbling, they were wispy and tall, wafting the air high above. But as we got close, touching their smooth legs, we could feel the breadth of their stance and knew their strength. We caught their leaves as they fell, thick and waxy. We slowed for a moment to rub them between our fingers, folding their crisp shapes in half, their scent warm and tangy. If

I had stopped to listen to those trees I may have heard them hushing, *pause... sit with us...*

The trees I loved. The running I hated. The mornings at altitude were cold and sometimes frosty, the air like glass. Running before breakfast I protested with cramps and cold, nose running, stomach blazing. Now I wish I had stopped to make more of it. Now I remember it as beautiful.

My friendships as a child were as deep as I knew how and I was fierce in my protection of them. I am told that I would focus on a drawing or a song with unusual intensity, then move on to something else as if I had been holding my breath and needed to come up for air. I loved to learn and would read and read, inhaling the words, racing through the pages. I wanted to know and learn and master things, to be at the end before I'd got started. Everything was interesting. Anything could be created, changed, imagined. The world was knowable and I wanted to be caught in its complexity.

There are tipping points, I think. Where a good thing is amplified into a concentration that becomes harmful to human ingestion. My ferocious appetite to know tipped from focus and delight, to control and defense. Joy in learning shifted to the satisfaction of having learnt it. Happiness in creating was smothered by the urge to have it completed. I was ruled by the need to finish at a pace and achieve more. I never made time to stop and stretch, relieve the tension, to allow for recovery and build strength. I imagined I was full of energy, but really I was living on adrenaline, even at rest. A walk was pleasing because it was accomplished. My mind was not out among the trees or in the wind, it was tethered to my noisy and demanding lists. My breath was thick with emergency. A cancelled train or a harsh comment would send a volt of cortisol, an amp of adrenaline, across my chest and down my arms. I revelled in the momentum and urgency of it all. I had no idea that my 'normal' was bound so tightly.

A weariness began as a slow creep and spread, a mist that never truly cleared. Everything came to be an effort. Cooking became a complicated series of unmanageable steps. Conversation was confusing. Music was too loud. All the activities I once enjoyed, I didn't. Excitement was cerebral. My body gave me nothing. No emotions, no butterflies, no thrills or laughs. Just blank.

Thirty years of living at a sprint will catch up with you. Your body will say *enough is enough* and your mind and soul will breathe a secret sigh of relief even as they crash. Now I see that I was hurtling towards a wall, with no idea how solid it would be.

*

Almost two decades later, and six thousand miles away from the eucalyptus trees and their whisper, my running shoes are worn in. I run to chat, never alone. My friend matches my pace easily and only when we have stopped to squint at our timer does she admit the strain. Not me. I sputter and complain all the way around the harbour waters. Everyone always knew I hated running. My third half-marathon did not go well. I started out sluggish, my brain lagging on the road behind me, every step an immense effort. I finished with a temperature and a bone-deep ache. *Just a bug*, I thought, and tried to shrug it off, but it hung there and thickened as the weeks went by. I put my running shoes away.

I had tests. Lots of tests. An ultrasound, a gastroendoscopy, and a barrage of blood tests culminating in a trip to the haematology department. I waited for results in the strange room that was laminated with a false cheeriness. The efficiency of nurses seemed to power the harsh electric lights that hummed across the low ceiling. As the weariness deepened the room got smaller. All I could see was the chair in front of me and the thin rectangle of an open door. I felt like I was deep underwater, compressed to a singularity point. Eventually there came a diagnosis by elimination: *Chronic Fatigue Syndrome.*

Nobody really knows why or how it happens, or how to treat it, but I knew the collapse it caused in my body. CFS sits on a spectrum of fatigue. The body stops creating energy in the usual way and leaves you exhausted. It feels like someone has taken your batteries out. Like you are cashing checks your body can't pay for, and the negative balance is painful.

My world constricted. I was signed off for three weeks, which turned into an indefinite future. I had to use both hands to lift a glass of water and lie down after the effort of brushing my teeth. Occasionally I would sip tea with a friend, talking slowly with my eyes shut to help me think. They would leave when my head began to droop onto my shoulder, my neck unable to keep it upright. My body was in revolt and all I could do was surrender to it and wait. I spent so much energy hating running. Now that I can't run, I miss it. *Will I ever run again?* I think. Who knows.

And so I lay on my bed and felt nothing. And thought nothing. And I breathed out. All the way out. And in the hiatus, I waited.

So this is pause... I thought.

*

I began to listen to the world around me: the radiator noises, the cars passing, the neighbors moving about on either side of our terraced flat. To the world inside me: temperature, heartbeat, breath, face-ache, shoulder tension. My base level, when everything was quiet, when there were no pressures or expectations, felt motionless. A still pool of water. My body was at rest. My mind was learning to lie still under the weight of a dark night. Even with the nausea, sensitivity to light, memory loss and isolation, there was a very small center of quietness. Everything was gone, except my empty body and empty mind. As I lay there, I felt a question rise from the depths and hang low over me. *What are you doing here?* it said.

Unable to do anything except wash and eat, I finally grasped the true value of life. I knew it in my heartbeat and in the rhythm of my breath. That central core, that beautiful human thing. My self; my soul. I was no longer the person I had always thought I was. This, then, was something to hold on to. Somewhere to start from. If I am no longer the adjectives I was, then who am I?

If I never get better, if this is my world, am I ok in it?

This understanding was not romantic or exciting. And its realization is painful and slow. But, in some strange and unaccountable way, I had never felt so good.

*

Time became distorted in my small world. With no distinction between the days, I lived just one at a time. And time passed, in the end.

My legs gradually returned beneath me and I walked across the park opposite with a small ache in my throat keeping my eyes in check. It felt wonderful. My wasted muscles were stunned into movement I thought they'd forgotten. So delicious, the knowledge of my body, the reluctance and eagerness to move again.

With everything stripped back, I begin to emerge. I can put back what is worth putting back and declare the rest no longer mine. My thinking feels different. Less linear and more connected, less categorized and more understood. Things shift with a shimmer of energy, of possibility, underneath. There is a pleasure in small things that I have not experienced before. I practice gratitude as a discipline, messaging a friend with tiny progresses, trying to #celebratethesmallstuff. Because the small stuff is what the bigger stuff is made of.

The thing about living at speed is that things become blurred as they flash by. Emotions are reduced to the big three: Happy, Sad, Angry.

Activities are finished or unfinished, fun or boring. Nuances are lost. The spectrum becomes binary, one thing or another. Conversation becomes immobile, thinking becomes rigid. The wide expanse of possibility is made small. I have found in slowness an abundance where I expected scarcity. A flexibility within limitations.

I began to think again. To hold a thought and allow it to germinate, to morph, to grow. To hold two thoughts and allow them to merge and multiply. To realize that the aim was less to come to an answer, and more to find the right question. Right in the very center of this strange and difficult time I wrote in my blue notebook: *These are the Glory Days.* This I must remember.

I Just Do One Thing. No multitasking, no efficiency. There is an unexpected detail in the everyday: getting dressed, the feeling of clothes moving over my skin, the gentle weight of blue wool across my shoulders. The soft ordinariness I had missed in the layers of rush, in the compression of hurry.

CFS created the context for a new beginning. I have been razed to the ground. My body and soul have been rested and nourished. Forced into both. I have been trapped in a dark tunnel and then brought out into a spacious place, where everything is gone. It is terrifying. But it is liberating.

The question is: *Can I now construct a life without the wall?*

*

There is a Georgian park near our flat with a small lake and sloping grass, well loved by the homes around it. There is, down one side, a long avenue of trees that lace their trailing fingers together overhead. Benches mark the path at intervals, and as I walk, the leaves above me hush and say, *pause... sit with us.* And so I do.

The canopy is wide above me as I sit, breathing in the light under the sky. As life begins again, and my body remembers how to love, and my mind clicks in, and my emotions roll around, the spiny wall of my own stress flickers and buds. I will not feed it or nurture it. But neglect is how it ravaged me before. I must not allow it to return.

Although these years have been slow-motioned, my self remembers old habits and bends towards acceleration. To combat it I must lean into the opposite, and so I make it my serious practice to linger. To remember my blue notebook and its moments. To ruthlessly eliminate hurry from my life. To enjoy. To feel.

The weight of the wall is lifted, its solidity eroded. My undoing was the beginning of things. And the aftermath of recovery, though long and hard, spells freedom.

ANN MARIE MEEHAN

The Low Door in the Wall

"But I was in search of love in those days, and I went full of curiosity and the faint, unrecognized apprehension that here, at last, I should find that low door in the wall, which others, I knew, had found before me, which opened on an enclosed and enchanted garden, which was somewhere, not overlooked by any window, in the heart of that grey city."

Evelyn Waugh, *Brideshead Revisited*

Elizabeth, New Jersey, is the armpit of the Garden State. It squats low astride the New Jersey Turnpike near Newark Bay. Rows of duplexes with vinyl siding flanks hunker over breezeways filled with the smells of jerk chicken and sauerkraut. Upon moving in, you notice that the windows of these homes are sealed shut. Like your neighbors, you sacrifice sun and air for privacy. Within your walls you can hear the strumming movement of everyone and everything escaping sad Elizabeth. Amtrak trains scream through, desperate for New York City, and choppers chuck-chuck through the polluted yellow sky, headed for the nearby trauma center. It was here that Thomas and I began our married life, in a second floor apartment on Washington Avenue, beside an untended graveyard and Luby's Bar.

I met Thomas when I was sixteen; he was the gnarled tree I swung to when my parents' marriage crumbled. He was puckish, with lichen-colored eyes; short but curiously tall. His head tilted to the right and his spine sunk to the left as if to balance him out. In his early twenties, he traded his Beatle boots, electric guitar, and rock for Irish traditional music and mandolin. When I met him he already had a wealth of jigs and reels in his head and always seemed to be at the epicenter of a great pub session.

Like a burr, I fastened myself to him. We spent that summer together in Hilltown Marbray's thirty-two pubs filled with music, dance, pints of porter, and local characters telling stories beside turf fires. It was his last year in Ireland, before he emigrated and married me to get a green card.

Thomas kept his corners dark. Occasionally, he'd disappear for days and wouldn't say where he'd been. And there was that black and white photograph in his family's sitting room of a crooked man standing in a graveyard beside a casket, surrounded by umbrella-wielding mourners. Clad all in black, the man is wearing dark sunglasses and white gloves. One arm salutes while the other balances a rifle against his shoulder.

In these early days, I pushed aside a deep, niggling feeling that my interest in him outweighed his interest in me. I'd been there before: I was the thick-thighed girl with the limp brown braids who chased the boys running after the blond, knob-kneed girls. I ran past nice towards handsome and talented and ignored warning signs. Although Thomas had many acquaintances, he had only one or two friends. At twenty-eight, he was still living at home with his parents and adult siblings. Three times a day, he ate Mammy-cooked meals in silence, across from a father he hadn't spoken to for years. But I chose to overlook these things, and so I ended up cooking his three daily meals in Elizabeth.

*

In the winter of 1982, I sat in darkness before our T.V. Thomas was working night shift, spray-painting newborn Cadillacs on an assembly line. I was glad he wasn't home; he hated all things English, especially T.V. dramas, and I was planning on watching "Brideshead Revisited," what he called "one of those awful Brit costume things." He'd driven off in his shabby Monte Carlo with the dinner I'd packed him, and donned his lead-tainted coveralls in the plant's men's room, racing to get to the line without getting docked for lateness.

I was watching Charles Ryder, protagonist and narrator, standing before crumbling Brideshead Castle, recounting his story of lost youth, lost loves, failed marriage, infidelity, and that "low door in the wall" he'd found at Oxford. His toneless voice seemed to bore into the emptiness of Elizabeth, making me feel as if I'd missed my own door.

I'd left La Salle in my sophomore year, vowing to get my Bachelor's someday. I had a lousy job at a nearby bank processing center where an assembly line of miscoded checks awaited my correction. Each night I'd return home, hoping Thomas had lit the kerosene heater to warm up the place up, only to find it cold and in darkness.

"Buy the pickle and pimento loaf. It's cheaper than the ham," he'd say as I prepared for my weekly run to the Acme while he headed for Luby's Bar to down as many mugs as he could before he left for work.

I sank into our low-slung, second-hand couch, wondering why he wouldn't let me drive the Monte Carlo to the store. "Gotta save on the gas," Thomas said. He pocketed the keys, squeezed a ten-dollar bill out of his full wallet, and handed it to me to put in my empty one. This was not the soft, cocoon-like marriage I'd imagined; this was all corners, edges, and ledges. I took stock of the small living room before walking to the Acme: one fetid, velvet couch and matching arm chair, a T.V., and a kerosene heater. From a point of great distance measured in decades that T.V. has taken on the appearance of a flotation device. I see that twenty-one year old me hugging it tight, searching the horizon for a life-boat.

I remember the first time I had that T.V. to myself: it was the day Diana married Prince Charles. She was an ardent young woman, lacking in worldliness, doing the same thing I'd done the week before: marry a reluctant, older man. It took me ten years to convince Thomas to leave Elizabeth for Philadelphia and my family. By then, Di and I were mothers and two forlorn women, living on the outer edges of our shrinking selves. Standing in a supermarket check-out line, I'd spot Di on the cover of a magazine, wearing the bottom half of a bikini top on a yacht beside a handsome man who was not Charles.

In this tenth year of my marriage, I, too, gave up and embraced infidelity. I was fed up with trying to convince Thomas that I was worthy of his love. This marriage wall was too high; I was losing my foothold. Creeping in secret, I squeezed my trim, white belly through that key hole and into Eden to writhe as one with someone else.

By the way, that door mentioned in Brideshead really exists. It's a dark green door at Christ Church, Oxford, that opens onto a secret garden behind walls of Cotswold stone. Lewis Carroll knew it well; a shrunken Alice fits through it after downing the contents of a bottle labeled "Drink Me." I always promised myself that someday, I'd write about that door that to me symbolizes escape for those engaged in social behaviors often considered outside the norm.

I decided to have an affair the year I lost forty pounds, after Thomas told me through his nightly haze of alcohol, "You've let yourself go. Do you think I'm going to want you if you keep gaining weight?"

Our marriage had become a whiney, ornery 'tween whose voice is cracking. Our children would crank up the volume on the T.V. to drown out our fights. I'd watch Thomas's mouth move and hear instead Roger Rabbit's manic, panic-shouting voice. If I looked like Jessica Rabbit would he be able to love me? I was embarrassed and ashamed that I couldn't seem to lose weight on my own, so I told him I wanted to join a weight loss program. But Thomas still had power of the purse.

"How much is this going to cost me?" he whined, when I told him. "I should have married an Irish girl!"

In the end, it cost us six-hundred-and-twenty-four dollars. Fifty-two weeks, twelve dollars a week. I attended every meeting and recorded everything that went into my body in a journal. I took up bike riding. For the first time in my life, I was a size ten. To my bewilderment, Thomas was enraged. His scorn was now at war with my new-found confidence.

"You think you look sooo great," he'd hiss, squeezing my wrist. "This was supposed to be about increasing my desire, not about you feeling better about yourself."

"Isn't this what you wanted?" I asked, standing before him in spandex, ready for my nightly ride.

That nightly ride. Salvation and sanity. Astride that narrow seat, I shed "wife" and "mother" and became "Bike-woman," whipping around streets on my second-hand skeleton of a racing bike, watch-less and helmet-less, in the age of the pager. If it hadn't been for that bike and the pager, I would have never escaped through that low door.

My co-conspirator was also a bike enthusiast. He had a pager, a truck, and a truck-bed big enough to toss two bikes into. We'd pick a rendezvous point and ride together, laughing, eyes flashing, driving fast, dangerously close, adrenaline and desire rising with our perspiration.

We met at work. The place where many sad, lonely, bored, hungry humans meet.

The phone calls came first. That delicious ache when you look down at the display and see his number. He was somewhere, thinking of me, wanting more of me who was stimulated by my confidence and appearance and sneering at Thomas's inability to love me. Lately I'd started noticing something odd about Thomas: He seemed to be shrinking.

We both stood five foot six inches, but ever since my transformation, I'd been lowering my gaze to meet his.

The lovers continued their impossible meetings aided by logistics and lies. Atop a stool at Smokey Joe's, she sipped gin and tonic, levitating off her stool when she spotted him walking through the door. His tweed jacket tugged at his muscular frame and his head jerked, jay-like, as he scanned the bar. His eyes landed on her and he was smiling at her and her desire, balanced upon the stool. Their conversation diffused in time, into their now. They were just two people with no provenance, linked only by their appetite for each other.

It didn't last a year, but that was long enough for me to imagine myself without Thomas. I felt stalk-straight, core-solid, restored. Adultery was a lubricant, the grease that eased me out of a rusted relationship, into a space that fit my changed self. All that biking and ardent loving and sloughing off Thomas and our marriage made me eager to scale the wall and throw myself over.

But I hung on a little longer to that ledge; our children were young and Thomas had reluctantly agreed that we give counseling a try. In the car on our way to our first visit, he cautioned me: "Now, here are the three things we're not going to talk about." Those were the three problems on the top of my list. We got nowhere.

"I don't love you anymore," I said, hoping he'd protest.

"I guess you're going to take all my money, right?"

Like Di, I'd always sensed there was a third party in my marriage. I just didn't expect it to be money. That night, he threw me up against the bedroom wall by the neck in front of our children. This earned me a protection-from-abuse order. Within a year, we were divorced.

After my divorce, I watched my children crawl out from under the rubble of our marriage. And I allowed myself to revisit my childhood and the low doors my parents used to escape their marriage.

My father built his wall of karst and enticed young boys to climb through its low door. I imagine my father as a tortured Grendel, impounding himself within this castle keep. Stony blades like shark fins run along the top of his wall. His is not a wall to take refuge in; it's a wall designed to sink one's monster self into, to stew in silent loathing of one's horrific side. To hide away from his daughter's eyes that I squeezed shut when I saw what I saw when I was in my teens. When I saw my dad gaze at young Bradley Fillmore's sweet peach-fuzzed upper lip with such intensity.

If my mother was jealous of my dad's construct, she shouldn't have been. Her wall was the Great Wall of China, buttressed with obstinacy, capable of withstanding any siege. She hadn't constructed hers to contain her secret affair; she built it to protect herself from my father's secret. Her garden contained a deep, Narcissus pool where she went alone to refresh and re-store herself, to forget her pederast husband. Through my childhood and teens, I danced and teetered and waved to her from atop her wall, trying to get her attention, just like I did with boys. Then I found the hand-written erotic poems, hidden in her vanity. I read them in the bathroom behind a locked door, knowing she hadn't written them for my father.

My mother immigrated to Ireland when I was eighteen to live with Stu-art, her lover from Hilltown Marbray. She strode out through our front door, hand in hand with him, chin in the air. I knew Stuart; he was an acquaintance of Thomas's. He was also the monster who grabbed me in a dark, empty pub one night when I was seventeen.

"Mom, I've got to tell you something before you do this. Stuart made a pass at me."

Her eyes became slits and her lips were fused together; she was as angry as I'd ever seen her.

"You're lying," she spat.

That was the day I constructed my wall to keep her out. This wall has held for forty years.

Just one last story of my family and walls.

It was summer and the sixties and everything was mod, groovy, heady, and sexed up. America, unleashed, was running like a rabbit in heat through Woodstock and Vietnam. Our house smelled of Lemon Chicken, Genoise cake, and cleaning fluid. The Mamas and Papas were dreaming of California on the radio. My parents swept about in brocade caftans, Mom doing all the work and Dad doing nothing and standing in the way, as usual.

My parents were hosting a grand dinner party for the McPhees, the Silvios, the Hogans. and my father's cousin, Brother Francis, a Jesuit on loan for the summer from his road-less parish in Guatemala.

I was setting out the silver, enjoying the feel of alternating hardwood and Persian rug on my bare soles. My mother's waist-length hair was cinched in a tight knot, stuck with chopsticks. I was relieved; her loose hair swaying above her ass always made me uncomfortable. I was nervous about Dad. What if the guests laughed at the gold medallion resting upon his rust-colored chest hair? He'd laugh, I thought. He was good at laughing.

In came the guests, hugging and kissing. The room grew close and tipsy with anticipation. Caruso's voice snaked out of the Victrola's black trumpet. Rivers of white and red wine flowed round the table and into Waterford glass.

"Please say the blessing, Frank," asked my mother, eager to carry in the platter of corn-starched, saucy chicken breasts.

Brother Frank smoothed his page-boy haircut in place and raised the leaden goblet before his wire-rimmed specs. He prattled through the items on his thanks-be-to checklist, anxious to get to the wine.

A high- pitched scream shot off the four walls like a pinball. My younger sister, Lee, was shouting and pointing at the sideboard table. Despite painstaking efforts to prepare for the party, my parents had overlooked something. The aquarium containing our two gerbils remained in the dining room, sitting atop the sideboard, its glass walls slicked with blood. Somewhere between setting the table and Father Frank's toast, father gerbil had made a feast of mother gerbil's litter.

Brother Frank, deep in his draught, had bitten down on the glass, his tongue bleeding profusely. Guests were fleeing, sickened; someone was waving one of my mother's linen napkins at Brother Frank's bloody mouth like a flag of retreat. My mother was on the verge of fainting, and my dad was finally doing something.

"JESUS!" whooped my dad. "Ooooooooo, JEEZ-US!"

He hoisted up the aquarium and ran through the kitchen, out the back door and across the lawn like it was on fire, frantic to find some dark corner of the backyard to hide the carnage contained within the aquarium's walls.

This marked the lowest door in our family history. I've labeled it "filial cannibalism."

KATHLEEN LANGSTROTH

The Door

I'm not really into blood. You know those who are always going on about the latest horror film or thriller? They would queue up to see the insides of anything exposed. Not my kind of rush really. But when you find blood decorating your home in unusual ways, the whole genre takes on a new enigmatic quality that invites revision.

I have to say that particular deep shiny red looks pretty damn nice on my pristine white walls. You need to take it out of context I suppose. I had been tempted to leave the splodges but that just wouldn't do. The pattern I found on the shower curtain was a surprise. Thought it was all cleaned up, but now this particular remnant serves as a kind of (perverse, would we call it?) souvenir of the event. Unfortunately, the lush crimson has transformed into a dead rusty brown, so not as aesthetically pleasing. Shame.

The whole scenario rates as significant enough to declare an 'event,' but not so much of a kerfuffle that it becomes an 'incident' in some official's notebook. I don't think. But no one was there. Just him and me. It even crossed my mind to take a picture of the door jamb and send it to someone. In the end, I couldn't think who to send it to, so I didn't do anything but clean up. There was a kind of beauty, I have to say. But to admit that would raise too many eyebrows in way too many places. I believe that would put me on the radar of those outside of this house. I shall keep this under my hat so to speak. Can I seriously consider following my instincts with even a surfeit of trust? Not entirely certain.

Ah well, it's all over now. He's fine. I'm fine. Thanks for asking. All the excitement is over. But there's always the possibility—expectation, if I'm honest—of another 'event'. Who knows what tomorrow will bring. *Que sera sera.*

The plate smashed into substantial chunks. We are talking about stoneware here. A formidable bulk that initially hesitates—an almost tangible pause before submitting to breaking apart and then only into large nuggets. I actually kept one of the pieces. I'm not sure how to explain that decision, if it's discovered. But this tiny sculpture, this fragment, has such a serene pastel glaze covering its curved surface. The cream-colored edges are revealed shyly. It couldn't do any damage normally but with some determined consistent pressure behind it, flesh would indeed buckle. A bit like teeth excavating corn niblets from a fresh hot buttery cob. Not that I dwell on it too much. It's just there on the tabletop tucked in behind a stack of books. Just in case I need it for something. There is a whisper of temptation there. Can't quite explain it.

He's in his room now. Behind the door. Although the hinges are under considerable strain. Not entirely certain that I can fix it when it comes off again. I will need to completely reframe the door this time. I'll deal with it when I must. I would have to say my feelings about doors have altered in interesting ways. I don't think people ponder doors generally. It had been a reassuring thing for me, the door. I think everyone could agree on that. You come home, close the door, you are safely folded into your cozy homestead. All nicely tucked in. When you have kids, there is that standard cliché moment when you say goodnight, bow out of the room, toggle the overhead light off and nestle the door into a closed position. The sense of completion is notable and satisfying. Freedom for the good parent to relax for the evening.

An open door is meant to be welcoming, isn't it? Not so much when he comes at me with venomous anger in the form of a raised fist. No. Or the strangle grip. I didn't get the door closed quickly enough last time. He had me up against the wall at once. Amazing to discover your hidden talents at these moments. How instinct and adrenaline can combine forces to save your arse. So here I am. But back to the door...fine, if it's closed. A signal to be alert if creaking open. I really need to come up with a plan for fixing those hinges. The repeated slamming is taking a huge toll. I just can't be asked now. I'm so very tired suddenly. I will need to rely on my quick thinking some other time. I had better rest up when I am able.

I try to think back. When did his identity become anger? He was a good kid, you know. I used to call him my happy little bug. You know how you say all those cutesy things when kids are small? He learned to walk early. He would plod around the house proudly repeating, "One, Two, Tree!". His sagging diaper never slowed down his adventures. His sisters tried to capture him and lift him up, giggling the whole time. He was too heavy for them and they always gave up. "Let's play hide and seek. You count... one...two...TREE!" The video footage replays in a loop in my mind every day now. Smile. Giggle. Toddle. Hug.

So how could I, his mother, consider dropping him off at the hospital, giving up my responsibility, admitting defeat? Well, I haven't done it yet, so no accusations, please. The withering inside me is a full-time process now. I can feel it physically. I walk around with it, knowing it is growing out from my center. Day after day, it pulls me closer to the floor, to the ground, underground. If people could actually see my defeat, I might be arrested or attacked. Most unwelcome. Or perhaps it will be me who attacks. In fact, I have developed a strong fascination with blades lately. It's the strangest thing. I see the gleaming metal edge. I wonder about the nature of broken surfaces. I have a craving. But what would become of him? I suppose I would need to drop him at the hospital beforehand.

It'll be interesting to see how this pans out. I mean, perhaps I should have left him at the hospital back when he was born. Now there's a thought: Give up before you even start. Well, no more time for luxurious contemplation. Time to act somehow. Up those stairs to that door. Grimace. Flinch. Growl. Clench.

TYLER DUNNING

—————

One Assumed Word

I'm fairly certain Francesca is trying to tell me about diarrhea. Our language barrier is the problem, the duck we both ate earlier in the day at lunch, where we met, the impetus for the diarrhea she is trying to confess. Or the diarrhea she is trying to accuse me of having—I'm just not sure. But now, a full twelve hours later, sometime near two a.m., we're on the prowl for food again, having fled a friend's afterparty due to rumors of kebab appealing to our late-night marijuana high, only to fail—the snow-kissed streets of Turin, Italy, empty of vendors—with us carrying that defeat back to the sixth-floor flat, flight after flight of steps, with Francesca holding her stomach, saying something about the duck, and making a joke that is just not landing. She pulls me aside, now isolated from the four-person pack, looking for the right word. *Diarrhea*, I want to say to her. *You're trying to say diarrhea.*

I'm confident she wants me. To kiss. To get to know me. It's the way she stared straight at me all night during my performance, reading stories in English that she'd later confess to not understanding, but appreciating the passion behind them. Yes, I'm sure, she wants me . . . making me then wonder: *Why are we discussing diarrhea?*

*

I came to Europe with a rag-tag crew of entertainers on a DIY house show tour, several goals in mind: to see the world, to share my art, to meet someone. Because to feel known and wanted by another human, to appeal to their greater senses as an object with worth that is deserving of time and attention, was all I really wanted as an artist. To feel interesting in another's presence, and to have that interest manifest as a burning in our loins that can't be controlled, hands touching places we don't let hands touch, mouths not for speaking—no language barrier—but for communicating a deeper urgency in our animal instincts: to lose our bodies in a place we have traveled so far to feel found—

It's difficult not to daydream of sex when abroad.

Francesca becomes my proof, a young woman who sat next to me during the middle of my meal with friends, the restaurant small and harboring no qualms of putting strangers at the same table. The handsome man Francesca is with sits across from us. I am despondent in the moment, feeling isolated from my own group, more of a spectator to their conversation than a part of it, so I am drawing, like a child, on my placemat: a human heart with a leafless winter tree growing up and through it, branches as if veins, trunk an aorta.

Francesca takes notice, making small talk, and I am so attracted to her spiraling mane of black hair I can't help but imagine my fingers running through it. Had she known I was using doodling to hide my sulking she would have dismissed me, but I'm quick to ask her to draw as well: a map, I suggest, of Italy and where she comes from. *Sardinia*, she tells me, *an island. You'd love it there.* And I want to kiss her, but, instead, invite her to our show that evening. That's when my Italian friend Piero steps in, as a proper wingman, and divulges the directions to his house in their native tongue. She says she'll come, as a promise, all of us then finishing our mozzarella, raw hamburger, and gnocchi with duck—oily and unctuous.

Hours later, my crew is getting drinks, just before the show, me and the boys plus a few others from the Camino de Santiago, and I've had just enough to be a true idiot, confessing that I want Francesca at the show, boyfriend or not, and that if he does come, I say in jest, I hope he's into cuckolding. This becomes problematic for the Italians, not because of the word's connotation, but again, translation issues. I spend the rest of my beer explaining, the best I can, what it means. One woman, newly met, looks horrified.

*

Francesca is the first to arrive at the show, no boyfriend in tow; in fact, she was on a first date that afternoon and confesses there won't be another. Therefore, somehow, this beautiful Italian woman only has eyes for me: the drunk, false-poet from lunch, cartooning like a kid, with a belly full of duck.

I perform well. Francesca stares. I relish the attention.

So now, alone in the stairwell after leaving the afterparty, an awkward framed photo of Nicki Minaj overlooking us, Francesca has since abandoned the recesses of her memory and is using Google to translate, she and I mere inches from touching: I can no longer tell when it's an appropriate time to kiss a girl. So, I just watch the phone load, concerned for the outcome: diarrhea, I'm sure of it. But her face enlightens, and she has solved the conundrum. *Digestion!* she exclaims to me. *Digesting that duck is making it hard to get up all these stairs!*

And she's laughing, moving in closer. But we've lingered too long. And I'm certain, now, that this is not the right time to kiss a girl, having navigated that thin space of a missed connection, one assumed word having built the barrier. I look at her confused for more reasons than just bowel movements.

We head back into the flat, into the throng of drunk Italians dancing erratically to American music that we, as Americans, have never heard. We dissipate in the crowd and all night long, through a cloud of pot and body odor, I see Francesca still staring, smiling. I smile back, trying to translate my own muddled instincts: this feels like love, yet I know that's not the right word for it—

And I've lost her again to the crowd, the moment of possibility having passed—the two of us just hungry strangers drawn to a placemat heart. The two of us, like snow, just outside the landscape window, still falling on the empty streets of Turin, Italy, and melting before we could ever dream of taking hold.

JAMES THOMPSON

———

My Father's Wall

My father shares a room with another man, but he's alone when I walk in. He's in his wheelchair next to the full-length mirror on his closet door. He stares at the mirror and reaches out his good left hand to touch the image. He presses his palm flat against the unyielding firmness of the thing and frowns. I think, That's what his life must be like, trying to touch your own reflection.

He sees my image and pulls his hand away quickly to turn his chair to me. His smile is the same radiant greeting without the loving salutation he can no longer voice. I pull up a chair and ask, "How are you doing, Dad?"

He nods and shrugs his shoulders. The nurse brought me up-to-date on his condition before I came in—at least as far as they can ascertain it from their side of the invisible wall surrounding him. I can only imagine the sea of words dammed in by his many strokes.

I tell him the latest news about my wife, our children and his grandchildren. I can read the pride in his face and he seems to sit more erect in the wheelchair. All his family are far away except for Jan and me. We're the only visitors he gets, and we can't come that often.

"I've got a treat for you, Dad," I say as I take his glass and fill it with ice from his ice bucket. I move to his bathroom and pour in a tiny bottle of his favorite Bourbon. I noticed his brand as the flight attendant rolled her cart down the aisle on my last business trip, and I bought all she would sell me. I top it off with tap water and bring it back to him.

His eyes light up as he notices it isn't just water. I place the glass in his good hand, and he moves it eagerly to his lips. He takes a long drink, consuming half the cocktail and hands the glass back to me. The glow on his cheeks tells me it's been a long time since his last drink. He smacks his lips to tell me it tasted good. He finishes the drink in two more sips and nods his head in appreciation. I stick the empty bottle back in my coat pocket. The nurses need never know of the forbidden fruit he consumed.

A nurse comes to his door. "Time for dinner, Mr. Thompson."

She moves to take command of his chair, but I intervene. "I'll take him down," I say.

I know his table. He sits with two other men whose walls are as thick as his. Each one sits tied in his chair with something like a bedsheet. I take the fourth position next to Dad.

"Do you want a meal, Mr. Thompson?" a waiter asks me.

"No, I'll eat later, thank you." The stuff is good for institutional food. It reminds me of the mess halls when I was in the Air Force. I wonder how much Dad can taste. Does his wall encompass his taste buds?

The waiter places a plate in front of Dad. I smile, noticing the metal side boards around the perimeter of the china. This is a new twist. It only means he's lost more control to the wall.

"Hey, Dad, at Thanksgiving dinner, you always said you wished your plate had sides. Now you've got them." I point to the walls holding in his meal. He picks up his fork and taps the metal retainers as he smiles at me.

Dad digs in with his good hand. Everything is bite-sized. There's no need for me to cut things up. He traps the morsels against the plate's walls quite expertly.

After the meal, I roll him back to his room. His new roommate is there, a widower like Dad, but much more vibrant, though every bit as old.

"Hi, Leonard," I say.

"Hello, Jim. How are you doing?" he asks.

"I'm fine. You and Dad getting along okay?"

"It's a good thing we both like sports. Your dad wants to watch anything in the way of sports, even boxing." He reaches out and punches Dad playfully on the shoulder. He turns on the TV and dials in an NBA game. Dad turns his chair to watch and soon becomes engrossed in the play.

Leonard pulls me aside and whispers, "I think your Dad's had more strokes lately. He doesn't seem nearly as responsive. I've only been his roommate for two weeks, but I can really tell a difference."

"Thanks, the nurse filled me in on that. They know he's had some mini-strokes, but there's nothing they can do for him, they say." I think it odd that Leonard can gauge the thickness of Dad's wall. To me, it's no different than after his first stroke, but I don't see him as often as Leonard does.

I stay for a while longer, until half time of the ballgame. I move to Dad and get his attention.

"I have to go now, Dad. I'll see you next week, okay?"

He takes my hand in his and nods his understanding. I say goodbye to Leonard and leave. I walk past the other residents, some dozing in their chairs and some who reach out to me and plead for my assistance in accomplishing their escape from the confines of the nursing home. At least Dad is resigned to his fate and remains stoic as always. I shake off my guilt at leaving him here. Jan and I could not care for him properly, and our home is not designed to accommodate an invalid in a wheelchair.

He's where he needs to be.

That night the phone rings at two in the morning.

"This is Dr. Morton at Sunny Manor. Is this Jim?"

"Yes, it is. What's the matter?"

"I'm sorry to tell you that your father passed away an hour ago. It was a massive stroke. There was no way we could warn you so you could be here for him. I'm sorry."

"We understand. Thanks, Doc. I'll call the funeral home."

Jan sits up next to me. "Was it about your father?"

"Yes. Dad's dead."

She puts her arms around me. "It's really a blessing for him."

I embrace her, "Yes, it is."

I call the funeral home and go back to bed. I lay there thinking about Dad. A massive stroke, was it? I know it was his last-ditch attempt to batter down his wall from within.

JENNIFER HOPPINS

———

Inside the Smiles of Men Not Meant for Me

Dawn. Rain rushes like a pounding waterfall over slick mountain stone. Droplets funneled through eaves tap a staccato beat, while a crow mimics the sound of a dry hinge. Our Aussie bolts toward the deck, eager to escape the downpour after his necessary trip to the back corner. In haste he slips on the sodden wood. One moment you're dancing, another, you're down.

As he plops his wet head on my lap, I wonder if I'm projecting embarrassment in his gesture, a motion that seeks consolation. Ozzie is so sensitive that it takes several encounters before he'll dare to approach a person with a tentative sniff, and this is always followed by a quick retreat. He's been dubbed "the chicken in a fur coat" but even our neighbor's free range brood is bold when it comes to people. He's not a sunny retriever, instant friend to all. He's afraid of unfamiliar people, the way I'm afraid of men.

Or rather, afraid of myself in the presence of men.

Attention, like rain, is a slippery surface. This rainfall in spring sends me sliding into a pattern, triggered by memories coded within the transition of seasons. Spring leading into Summer marks the first beat of my unintentional ritual, the anniversary reaction of my divorce. With humid temperatures and longer days of sunlight, I begin to feel pretty again, lighter and freer in my sundresses. Winter has passed, and out of the cave I walk, unguarded and giddy. If a random conversation occurs,

I smile and laugh easily, buoyed by the return of tree blossoms and white clouds. But later I wonder, did I give the impression of flirting? Are smiles harmless?

*

At home again, I ruminate while preparing sauteed onion with zucchini. Slicing the onion of old shame, my internal critic cuts through thin dry layers, finding the moisture that weeps within. Part of my anniversary reaction involves wistfulness about the idea being free. While the pan releases savory aroma, I switch on all the fans in the house. I switch on survival mode.

Since my divorce, I seek out mostly feminine friendships, and shy away from men. This is difficult in my new occupation as a playwright, where going to work means engaging with every kind of person of all gender, nationality, age or sexual preference. If an actor or director approaches, and they are male, my alarm bells start ringing. I worry that the openness that theatrical performance creates in me will carry over into conversation. Will something low and buried under the gravel inside the well of my need for attention and affection wake up like a needy monster? Will I become alive in a new way if a man makes me laugh? How then to mask this secret joy? Stuff down this floaty feeling? I am now married to a handsome man who meets my needs for love and who is devoted and kind. Because of him, I know love in a way that I've never known it before. He chooses to trust me. He honors me with this trust. He sees my former situation of falling in love with Blue in the light of compassion. For him my story is a story of a woman who needed to feel love because she was not loved.

I find it difficult to forgive myself. I fear that my truth is so tied to subjective feeling that no one will understand, least of all my daughter, who was deeply hurt by the results of my action. If my first husband were here to comment, his voice would remind me that this is also a story about man who was betrayed by a woman he didn't trust. Right from the start.

When your husband doesn't trust you, it means that you spend most of your life safely behind physical walls. You go to the grocery store, to the laundromat, to all the necessary and ordinary places, rarely independently, mostly with the baby. But the more insecurity he feels, the higher the tension rises, so even these drab places are to be explored with him firmly stuck to your side.

This rising tension of mistrust happens incrementally over a decade, barely noticeable until one day you wake up and realize that your life has become contained in a radius of five miles. Was it only his insecurity that created the mistrust, or the reality that I still held a well of unfulfilled desire, dreaming through the night that one day I would be swept away in a rush of love, consumed and consuming, transformed by nights of bliss?

All through my twenties, I coped with unfulfilled desire by reading paperback novels from the library. But that was not real connection. I still carried a need for adult conversation during those years of juvenile cartoons, years of irritating (to my ears) country music, wrestling on the television, and greasy frying pans to clean. On several occasions my first husband was invited out to parties, which he attended, but left me at home. I desperately wanted to go out, but he refused to include me.

Then out of the blue, a decade into my first marriage, I met the man who would become my lover for a brief time. I justified the lovely feelings by remembering afresh that raging fight, when my then husband blocked the door and threw my overnight bag across the room. The tickets my brother sent for *Les Mis* in Detroit? He refused to let me go, because our daughter was sick with a cold. Again I stayed behind the walls, but with a new boiling resentment to be so trapped.

So I slipped on the surface of male attention several years after that fight.

Blue was closing the gift shop. All the customers had driven away with bags of mulch and flats of petunias. As he clicked the light switch, I let him kiss me softly, thrilled with the way his hands slid up my sides, the way his lips met mine in gentleness. This kiss was a weed I should have pulled. An invasive rhizome of feeling I allowed to grow unchecked. I most certainly should not have allowed this elation to later be expressed in ink, carelessly leaving the letter that spoke my heart to Blue in a notebook while I showered for work. It felt like the end of the world was happening as I stood naked, the shampoo sliding down my shoulders, the curtain smashed open by my husband, my pages of love-drenched ink crumpled in his raging fist.

The fragments of my memory include a grab for my jean shorts during his fury. I yelled "oh God!" as he threw his shotgun into the trunk of his car. On impulse, he returned for our daughter. Snapped her into a seat belt. His tires squealed away. The shampoo remained stuck to my hair and scalp. My bare feet hit the sidewalk, bones pounding into concrete. I must warn Blue.

I slipped in the rain and for a long while, I didn't get up. Blue refused to worry, to meet me and take me somewhere safe. Instead he said, "Make it right with him. You don't want to do this to your daughter. He won't do anything stupid. He's just blowing steam."

I called my mother, desperate for rescue. Maybe she had been expecting this call. I told her everything and we cried.

Wait. I'm remembering this wrong. I cried, she was firm. Emphatic. I must make things right again. Continue to work on my marriage. Go to the priest. Confess my sin.

Instead of following her orders, I searched for a safe place to stay.

Two weeks later, my husband and daughter were home. The memory I reconstruct of my daughter at eight, tucked under her princess comforter, is one of painful tenderness. I see her expectant smile and bright eyes fall into confusion.

"When will you be back? Can I go with you? Why are you going away, Mommy?"

"Daddy and I cannot be together as husband and wife anymore."

"But why? You love each other. You say it every day!"

I don't know how to tell her this, but the words *I love you* are not always true.

"What did I do wrong? Why are you leaving?"

"You have done nothing wrong, nothing in the world."

If in that moment I possessed the courage to tell my eight-year-old child "because Mommy stupidly fell in love with a different man" it may have empowered us both.

I now believe it would have been wise to tell her the difficult truth, so that we could have dealt openly with a fact. In my effort to cover up my shame, vague phrases escaped my lips. Falling into cliché and passive fumbling, I offered, "Sometimes things just happen." What things?" Dare I say, "I am afraid of your daddy's rage?"

No wonder when she came to visit, she screamed at me. Fell apart sobbing. Kicked the back of the driver's seat while I drove around, waiting for her to find control. Kicking it so hard, she jolted me forward into the steering wheel. Wanting the answer I held tight.

Maybe the event of falling in love with Blue was merely the surface of a floating iceberg, and wouldn't have satisfied the entire reason for my leaving. Our years woven together as a family had unraveled slowly, one situation, one conflict at a time. A story too long to tell in one sitting. Or a hundred.

John O'Donohue says in *Anam Cara* "as your experience extends and deepens, your memory becomes richer and more complex. Your soul is the priestess of memory, selecting, sifting, and ultimately gathering your vanishing days toward presence. This liturgy of remembrance, literally re-remembering, is always at work within you." Seventeen years after sliding the key into the lock of my new apartment, I revisit that time when my new solitude as a separated woman became my healer and my agony. Alone, I waited for him. I hoped. I imagined reasons why he didn't. I begged God. I raged at God. I bargained with God, "Please let Blue come to my door."

I finally went to a priest and formally confessed my sin. And then later I recreated the map of my body as it felt under Blue's fingertips, just barely there on the soft surface of my waiting skin, his lips pressing into mine, the fantasy dissolving into empty air. I heard his silence in the flowers growing on my porch, the million-bells petunias we started together in the greenhouse where we once worked.

I craved repetition of the endorphin-drenched, sky soaring ride through the spectral universe. The feeling of being fully, awestruck-awake to shapes, sounds, activity, temperature, and texture around me. To the subtle transformation of chromatic variation in the evening sky. Tangibly experiencing the near- touch of his hands. Alert to the feelings almost spoken aloud, yet diverting language, dodging banality. Joking with one another, communicating expectant joy, blushing with tension and half buried anticipation, inside the secrecy of our protected silence.

It is an empty road filled with loss, the outward search for these feelings of electrified life, this elevated perception of aliveness, inside the smiles of men not meant for me. I now recognize these moments as the entrance to a trap. I pull weeds. Today I care less for the thrill of those fast-growing invasives that bolt upright, leaning toward the sun. They produce no fruit, while stealing precious nutrients from the soil. I've noticed that the more I risk going out into society, attending a reading, seeing a show, participating in a writer's group, male attention is still an occasional, surprising event. But I don't let it constrain me behind these domestic walls. I keep the feelings secret when they happen. And before too long, they dissolve like sugary candy on the rain drenched ground. I've learned to go within myself for this feeling of aliveness, waiting in silence until I become charged with hope, infused with light, even as the rain falls.

In moments of meditation and solitude I discover that living with trust requires me to recreate it in the moments of each new encounter. It's not something I am privileged to expect as a given from another person, even my beautiful new husband. The truth is that knowing my story, he might wonder if I am always true. I am learning to recognize the energy of curiosity. How it is a power that can break vows. A power to explode walls. My awareness of this curiosity sends me backward in time, to review a memory of pain that followed from the subtle smile of my lover. Awareness without action, awareness without response, awareness without wonder (who is that guy behind his killer smile?) All of this awareness sublimates my curiosity into self trust.

I wouldn't, perhaps, be human, if the smiles of men did not wake me up. Who am I to claim that I am completely immune to sparks of wit thrown my way? And what is the best way to handle it?

I have a good friend, a middle aged woman like me, who is in so many ways my opposite. She wears fantastic dreadlocks, a nose ring. She splurges on the best shoes. She pays all the bills and lives in an old log cabin in the center of the hood. Her job is to care for injured pit bull terriers, the ones who have been used for fighting. Just today she posted about an encounter with some guy standing in line at the dollar store. He said, "You are wearing those jeans. Those jeans are making my eyes water." She promptly turned and said the best and most powerful swear word, followed by "you." He said, "Geez, can't you take a compliment, lady?" And she said "One more word. One more word and I will throat punch you."

How I wish I had her power. Yet, that wish denies that, were I in her situation, I would have secretly liked what he said, and admired his boldness, no matter that it was disrespectful objectification. If I had felt degraded in the moment, there would have also contained, in the same breath, a tiny thrill.

Maybe it's not up to me to understand why. Maybe it is simply a matter of allowing that kind of energy, that floaty feeling, and using it to walk outside and notice the way the clouds are stacking up into mountains of white over a base of gray. Or using the energy to sit at my sewing machine and work out the unused tension. Or start shaping something out of nothing in the kitchen, chopping garlic, sizzling a mixture of herbs to build a wine sauce.

This has taken practice. It's an ongoing practice. I'm discovering as my family grows, there are more invitations that I am able to accept beyond the domestic pumpkin shell. After several visits to a writer's forum, I was invited to the pub for drinks. I texted my husband to let him know about the invitation, and that I would be later than usual. All the lights were on when I came home.

These nights are hard for him.

I don't think he *really* trusts me.

But I keep going out, anyway, trusting myself. And just last week, I invited him to join us. He had a wonderful time. He told me he understands why I like this group of people, mostly men, a few women. This creative life is made better when shared with the one you love. How wonderful to share not only parenting and chores, but that nerve-wracking feeling that comes when you offer a piece of your writing in a group setting.

It's critical to keep testing my resolve in social situations, knowing what happens to a family when mom never goes out. If it's because she's too afraid to learn how to relate to people in a safe way, she can become a sort of zombie who is only half-living through the stories she reads, the images on a screen, through the safe energies that cannot be touched, ever removed from live human contact. Terry Eagleton says in *The Nature of Evil*, "Desire is absolutely nothing personal and will pass all the way through its (purely contingent) object in order to finally reunite with the only thing it really desires, namely itself." I like this idea that desire can pass all the way through without my engagement, without my resistance, without meeting desire with desire. It can pass right through, a thing felt, but a thing to let go.

CARRIE PEPPER

———

Walls of Time

Wyoming. A place where no walls exist. Tumbleweeds tumble and bounce across dry, sage covered prairies, lodging against weathered snow fences, piling up like ragged balls of twine. The wind never stops blowing—reminding me how open and free and constant life comes at me—in my face, voices on the wind, nothing to stop them, no walls to confine or cast shadows. Overwhelming at times, all the space, no dividers to chunk things up, make life easier to deal with. Here, nothing is held back—spirits on the wind, cold and snow and ever-present space.

Walls are back there, in my other world, the world I keep returning to—walls safe to hunker down behind like Tony and I did there at 7020 Jefferson Davis Highway, Richmond, Virginia. We sat in cool night grass, our backs against the warm, concrete wall of our incinerator, the Peppers' family trash burning in the big grey block with the hole on top. As milk cartons melted and paper sacks turned to ash, floating up in wisps of black lace, Tony lit a cigarette. Safety here with the smoke, no one to know he was breaking the rules, just me, the little sister, and, with me, this sin was safe. One secret we shared as we sat, shoulder-to-shoulder, smoke rising, curling overhead while brother and sister sat in silence far away from a father's punishment.

We shared other walls too, Tony and me: the cinderblock garden wall I'd walk atop barefoot, balancing on narrow borders of big, rough, open spaces, until the day my pink baby foot slipped, plunging down inside the coarse cement hole, scraping flesh—tears and blood and my big brother's arms carrying me to safety, to the blue and white bathroom where my mother applied orange Mercurochrome against my wishes then wrapped me with gauze, my brother looking on from the hall. "He used to just sit and watch you sleep," she told me once. Our walls are now walls of time—fifty years since my blond-haired brother disappeared in a jungle halfway across the world.

If our walls were of concrete or grey cinder blocks we could scale—we *would* scale—them to be together, but the walls are walls of time, as tall as Heaven, and we are on opposite sides.

TRACEY YOKAS

———

What Walls Were

This can't be happening to us.

And yet it is.

It's 2014. I'm in bed and glance Olivia's way. She's there, across the hall, lying on her floor listening to her damn metal music and texting, like a million other fifteen-year-olds around the country. She's not crying or raging or slapping herself, and there is no weapon in sight.

I hear a *bzz-bzz.*

She picks up her phone and texts.

My God, I revel. *So normal.*

I am about to lean back when Olivia raises her left forearm off the carpet and runs her right hand to the bend in her elbow. Then a gentle flick of the wrist and I realize she has just cut herself.

My heart pounds as she lowers both arms back to the floor and dabs at the spot with a crumpled black T-shirt heaped in a ball beneath her.

I want to scream, *I can see you! How can you do this to us again?,* but I've been warned. Relapses are common. Slips happen.

Magical thinking convinced me my family would be different. We'd be lucky. When she stopped the cutting, it had been for good.

I freeze, watching, as she does it again, and do what I've been coached to do. I don't engage. I lean back against my headboard, out of her sightline. My limbs go leaden.

A litany of opinions and instructions cascades through my mind. *Cutting isn't as bad as you think. Yelling at her won't work. Don't get into a power struggle. If she wants to cut badly enough, she will.* I have a choice to make: To get up and say something as usual or turn away.

I cannot turn away.

I toss off the covers and walk across the hall.

"Olivia," I say, speaking louder than the screeching music, but not screaming. I've been trained not to go there.

She ignores me.

I kneel down and try again. In the calmest voice I can muster, and with the therapist's words ringing in my head, I say, "You're hurting yourself and you need to stop."

"No," she says. "I don't get to do this much anymore. Leave me alone and get out."

I pause. Seconds tick by. I have another choice to make. I can do what I've done over and over and persuade, beg, plead, punish, bribe, or abide stone-like beside her. Or not.

My body takes over, able to understand what my brain can't or won't. My words will never force her to make the healthy choice. Recovery is a decision she has to make for herself. At the end of the day, a sheet of drywall, some nails, and a coat of paint can keep out the elements, but not self-harm. Without another word, I stand and leave her and her razorblade behind.

It's taken everything I have to get to this point.

One year earlier, I sat in my home office. My husband, Tom, built the addition for me with his own two hands, as a labor of love. It's the room where I felt most safe. But that day, with Olivia at school, I was staring at my computer, wracking my brain. I was determined to understand and to learn enough about depression, eating disorders, and self-harm to fix her mental illness. I believed I could. Of course I could. I looked at her precious art: clay turkey, #1 MOM painted mug, plaster foot cast from kindergarten. This can't be happening to us.

And yet it was.

Why? What had I done wrong? It's a mother's job to keep her child safe, especially in her own home. What did it say about me that I couldn't? It seemed like five minutes had passed since we were cutting paper Christmas trees. How had scissors—and knives and shavers and pencil sharpeners and pushpins—become weapons? Was I part of the reason?

I ran a search for the words: "self-harm," "treatment," and "cure." Link after link lead me along the information highway detailing symptoms, treatment modalities, and etiologies. None of it made sense. Olivia hadn't been neglected or abused. Our family environment wasn't unstable. True, my mothering wasn't perfect. But whose is? I hadn't fallen that far short of my hopes and aspirations. Had I?

I clicked and ordered books and read articles. Words like "not usually suicidal" and "chronic feelings of emptiness," meant to educate, terrorized me instead. I had never known such fear. I had to find our safety again. As a mom, it was my job.

Olivia was the most perfect baby I could imagine, with her perfect fingers, perfect toes, and blue almond-shaped eyes. In those first weeks together, I felt a safety that I hadn't felt in years—a safety in this new thing called motherhood. In quiet moments with Olivia, I cradled my tiny treasure and promised to love and protect her. I vowed to create a stable home and family for her and did.

She had a mommy and daddy who doted on her and a cat nestled at the foot of her bed. She had a room overflowing with books and stuffed animals. Together, we colored Disney princesses, read *Leo The Lightening Bug*, and sang "You Are My Sunshine." Like me, she hated to be a disappointment and endeavored never to be one. We spoke and she listened, as I had with my parents. Home was where I wiped away Olivia's tears, patched up skinned knees, and smothered her in kisses. There were clothes to wear and food to eat. She thrived.

Olivia's circle grew to include friends. Safety was sleep-overs, nail polish, and fake tattoos stuck to the carpet. There was swim team and Girl Scouts. Our life was a billboard for security and stability. Everything was on track. Nothing breached our borders or threatened our refuge. Nothing, that is until mental illness hit.

At first, Olivia started skipping breakfast. She argued and swore.

"Watch your mouth," I'd say, chalking it up to teen hormones. But as the weeks passed, she ate less and less and was angry and sullen more and more.

I didn't want to overreact even though I was seeing my childhood all over again in my daughter. Something that I had never really confronted: body image issues.

Olivia's pediatrician had cautioned me about her weight as far back as her four-year check up. *She inherited a larger frame, just like me,* I'd thought, trying to assuage my guilt and shame with a lie. I'd dieted off and on since sixth grade, and was never happy with the results. The last thing I'd wanted was for Olivia to hear the repetitive parental soundtrack of my youth to eat less and exercise more. Now I wondered how far she was willing to go.

Olivia lost twenty pounds in two months. She was a stick. "I'm disgusting," she yelled into the bathroom mirror, seeing more of herself than was there. In place of playdates, she exercised in the privacy of her room and emerged drenched in sweat. I accommodated her food demands by eliminating added fats, reducing carbohydrates, and increasing veggie options and still had to coax her to eat one or two bites. When she relented and ate an entire banana, she said she hated herself.

Her pediatrician told her she had to eat to stay alive. Her father and I concurred. She scowled and ignored us all. Had I acted like that with my own parents? It felt like she was acting out by choice and threatening all that I'd created in our happy home.

One day after school I was at my wit's end. I burst through Olivia's bedroom door, intent on demanding she get her shit together.

She sat on the edge of her bed, surrounded by stuffed animals. "Get out," she screamed. Her eyes locked on mine. Her hatred took my breath away. "I hate you. This is your fault."

"Babe–" I moved toward her to offer a hug and sit down.

She sank to the floor and bashed her head into the thick wooden frame of her bed.

I lurched forward. "Stop!" I put my hand between her head and the bed.

We crumpled into a heap. "It's too hard," she sobbed. Her mascara smudged my jeans. I realized she meant life. Being alive was too hard. This wasn't typical teenage hormones or body image stuff. This was something more serious.

Our family began treatment, therapy, and interventions. But the harder we worked, the further she withdrew at home and at school. "Shut up." "Leave me alone." "Fuck off." A symptom of her illness. Any semblance of normalcy disintegrated. Doors slammed. Voices rose. Warnings bounced off the walls of our safe haven turned war zone.

I needed help.

I found a therapist of my own. Each week, I spilled the details of our life to Kim. Usually, I bawled.

"You know," Kim said. "Olivia wants to see you taking care of yourself."

"Are you kidding me? I can't. That's selfish. And at a time like this, aren't we supposed to be talking about Olivia?"

Kim just nodded, but she was right. I wasn't sleeping. I was eating too much, not exercising, lacked enthusiasm for anything. I withdrew from my friends, tethered to my computer or a book, or, when I could no longer think, the television. All I could focus on was Olivia. I lived in fear of her next skipped meal, her next breakdown, her next whatever.

Still, I tried not to intervene. Olivia needed time to fill her therapeutic toolbox with tools, And I did too. Kim was teaching me how to stay calm during Olivia's storms. How to slow my body movements, lower my voice, take deep breaths, meet Olivia at her level. "The more upset she becomes, the softer you become," Kim instructed.

It made sense and I tried it, but Olivia raged on.

"Why do you think she acts out around you?" Kim asked.

"I don't know. . .because she can?"

"What do you think that means?"

Silence.

"She trusts me?"

Kim smiled. "Yes. You're her safe place. She knows you'll always be there for her."

"I will." *But what about our home and Tom and our life? Isn't that her safety? Is it really me?*

Two months later, I heard the words no mother wants to hear: "I want to die."

A call to 911, daily attendance at a treatment center, a clinical team, medication.

"Please, Mom," Olivia said, trembling in anguish in her room. "You have to kill me. There's something wrong with me." She had accepted her illness. I couldn't. Instead, I held her. I tried to give her that soft landing place of motherly safety. I wanted to believe I could control her illness despite the dawning realizations that control isn't safety, that walls don't always protect.

That's when the blood arrived. So much blood.

Olivia cut and cut. Her blood was everywhere. I found it in her bed. On the floor. Down the drain. There were endless loads of laundry, purchases of long-sleeve shirts, Neosporin and Band-Aids. Tom bought a real toolbox, a fire-engine red Craftsman, and hid the sharps. He taped the Safety Plan-Emergency Number document next to the phone. I scoured every inch of her room for contraband. I stood sentry outside the bathroom door, sat vigil outside her bedroom door. Constantly on guard. No respite, until I succumbed to exhaustion and collapsed into bed. If my daughter couldn't enjoy life, neither would I. For a few brief moments, as I fell asleep, I felt a scintilla of freedom from the relentless guilt and despair—the only kind of reprieve available.

Hours morphed to days and rhyme-less, reasonless weeks. Any illusion of safety shattered. The container of our home and my motherhood couldn't cure Olivia. In order for heal, she needed different walls.

Residential treatment, involuntary psychiatric hospitalizations, more doctors and nurses.

More questions that no one could answer. Who would she become without me in the mix? Could I admit to a modicum of relief that it was
someone else's turn to stand vigil? Most of all, would they teach her
what I wanted most for her? To trust herself. Value herself. Love herself
unconditionally. Was my therapist right? Did I have to love myself first?

Two o'clock in the morning. The Emergency Room.

I leaned over the gurney and whispered into Olivia's ear, "Move over
babe." I climbed on next to her, careful not to disturb the glue holding
together fresh wounds. I wanted to stay inside this bubble forever. Here,
my exhausted child was safe. No other expectation about her life mat-
tered. Revolving doors of treatment, lab coats, and worried expressions
might be the sum total for her. Lying there, I had no choice left but to accept. Her illness. My powerlessness. The dissolution of my dreams, and
what that said about my family and me. I let go of it all. Olivia was safe
here. I was with her in this bloodless, sanitary, protected place.

Two weeks later, Olivia landed at another residential treatment center,
and that's where it finally happened. During one group therapy session,
we worked on a learning exercise called the Whole Person Wheel. A
circle on a piece of paper was divided into six equal slices. Each slice
was labeled with a human potential: spiritual, physical, social, emotional,
mental, and volitional. We had to color each slice to the degree that we
felt whole in that category. That's how we would measure our Self-Worth.

I chose the most concrete category first: the physical.

I conducted a mental scan from head to toe, pinpointing one imper-
fection after another, and grabbed a purple crayon. I longed to lie. I
wouldn't though. Lying to myself had contributed to this mess. I continued my work and set down my waxy tool.

There it was. In the white space. More white space than not. What I'd
been hiding behind my emotional and physical walls for so very long,

raw and exposed. Now, even those walls weren't safe.

I looked at Olivia's chart. It was almost identical to mine. I'd had no idea.

I finally understood what Kim was trying to clarify for me through our discussions: How can a mother who is uncomfortable in her own body teach her daughter to cherish hers? How could I expect my gorgeous girl to give to herself what I was unwilling and unable to give to myself?

Later, I told Kim, "I feel like a failure."

She cocked her head. "That's a lot to get from one piece of paper. What's the takeaway?"

"I've been going about this all wrong," I replied. "Women are taught to take care of others first. Especially moms. The system is backwards. I don't want that for Olivia

"Maybe it's time to let yourself off the hook and focus on what you can control. Taking care of you."

She was right. It took four decades, but there I was. The biggest mistake I made as a mother was not lavishing myself with the same love, acceptance, and trust I felt for Olivia. The one person whose suffering I hadn't deemed important to address was mine. Olivia was doing the work on herself. It was time to bring in the wrecking ball, break down my walls, and see what self-care was all about.

Nine months after the Whole Person Wheel, countless hours of personal therapy and self-care work, and three weeks after I left Olivia with her razorblade, I am in the living room watching television. Olivia is in her room.

"Mom, can you come here?"

"Be right there." *More trouble?* I round the corner.

She's in her bathroom.

"What's up?"

"I wanted you to see this."

"See what?" I glance around. No blood. No drips on the floor. No bandages in the trashcan. No stains on her sleeves.

Olivia tilts her head toward the toilet, and I peer inside. At the bottom of the bowl are three razorblades. She flushes, and we watch the blades float up, swirl around, and disappear from view.

This can't be happening to us. And yet it is.

We stand where our story began. Inside the walls of our home. I don't move. I don't breathe. I don't want to break the spell. I search for words, but which ones could be adequate to describe this moment? The relief. Excitement. Joy. Fear. The words *What if?* ring in my mind. Yes. This moment could turn out terribly wrong or perfectly right. Today, I choose optimism.

"Thank you for sharing that with me," I say.

She smiles. Maybe at me. Maybe at her hard work. But definitely at what we've built together: new walls of love and acceptance. For each other. For ourselves. That's where we're truly safe.

JENNIFER HUBBARD

The Wall of Fear

At the beginning of Shirley Jackson's *We Have Always Lived in the Castle*, villagers taunt Merricat Blackwood while she runs errands. Merricat cherishes revenge fantasies while outwardly trying to remain cool, to pretend none of it bothers her.

As a reader, I recognized this situation instantly—the mockery, the insults, the exclusion—having been bullied by classmates. I knew that solitary walk while inwardly plotting escape (Merricat imagines herself living on the moon; I just imagined myself in a nice peaceful place where nobody would come uninvited). I knew the bitter hopes that someday they would all suffer. I knew that sense of constant threat—will it happen today, how bad will it be, what will they do, how far will they go? Where will they stop; will they ever stop?

In my mind I walked the gauntlet of tormentors with Merricat, walked with her through the village to the edge of her family's fenced property, where she unlocked the gate and let herself in. She locked the gate behind her and set off down a woodland path. She was safely home.

How I envied her that gate, those locks!

Merricat's dark secrets, revealed later in the book, were not my own, nor did I share her belief in magic. But for a long time I dreamed of having a house with acres of wild land, and a fence to keep out dangerous people. Land that would nourish me, surrounded by a stout barrier against intrusion, against the insults and rejections and meannesses of people.

*

My classmates never harmed me physically, although I always worried that they would, because I had no trust in them and no control over what they might decide to do. But in my late teens and early twenties, physical safety became an issue in a new and real way. I lived in a city neighborhood where muggings and break-ins were not infrequent. It was common to have burglar bars on first-floor windows, so common that when I visited my parents in their suburban home, their unguarded windows disturbed me. Multiple locks, deadbolts, and iron bars had become my new normal.

Despite my precautions, I could not protect my space.

The burglar who smashed through the door of my city apartment tore the cover off my Bible (apparently many people keep money in Bibles, though I never have), jerked my mattress off the box spring (hunting for the money I never kept there, either), and spilled out a box of letters and cards. He took postage stamps, an old wristwatch, and the little bit of cash I'd kept on top of my bookcase. Small items, a desperate theft—items worth far less than the peace he wrecked.

I did have compassion for him, even as I surveyed the damage he'd left behind, the cards and letters strewn across the floor, the splintered doorframe. But my fear loomed far larger.

*

I strengthened my locks. When I moved up to the second floor, I had burglar bars installed on the windows and the door that led to my porch. I was not the only one in the neighborhood who had bars installed on second-floor windows, as burglars had begun to climb up porch roofs and attack the upper floors. The building in which I lived had at least three burglaries, and one night a prowler scrambled onto my porch.

Shortly after the night of the prowler, I moved out. The bars on my second-floor windows and porch door had not been enough to make me feel secure.

*

The world was always reminding me that even the largest barricades were not infallible. While I was still living behind my burglar bars, the Berlin Wall came down. I remember hearing on the news that the border was going to open up a bit, and an eye-blink later people were out there with hammers and chisels, knocking down the hated wall with their own hands, dancing atop the ruins.

In a book called *The Great Hedge of India*, I found another story of a disappearing barrier, Roy Moxham's search for any trace of a giant hedge that the British had installed across India in the 1800s to enforce the taxation of salt. Moxham found that time had nearly eradicated not only the physical hedge but even the memory of it. Long-forgotten references in old records, and one brief scrap of hedge, were all that remained of a once-imposing barrier. Nothing more.

*

People may give different rationales for walls built to keep people out and walls built to keep people in. Walls built to safeguard and walls built to oppress. The common denominator is fear. Barriers are fear made solid and visible, born of the desire for protection, for certainty, for safety. For the power to guard ourselves from harm both real and imagined. The common denominator is the desire to keep what we have, safe from anyone else who might try to take it.

Fear is emotional, elemental, self-protective. It doesn't obey logic or justice. In the grip of it, in its urgent quaking clutches, it's difficult even to question, let alone to overcome.

*

One night in her Oakland neighborhood, writer and urban farmer No-
vella Carpenter was surrounded by teens, one with a gun. Instead of
raising a wall of panic or aggression, she chose to talk to them—with
passion and compassion—about the dangers of guns, about the risks of
being armed on the streets. Whatever they thought of this lecture, they
let her go. This scene, recounted in Carpenter's book *Farm City: The
Education of an Urban Farmer*, would not necessarily end the same way
in every similar situation. There are no guarantees. But it points to other
possibilities, options beyond the usual cycle of fear and aggression.

It's incredibly difficult to respond to perceived threats with openness, to
offer connection when the desire is to retreat, to fight that urge to raise
the wall. Walls are easier, which is probably why we have so many of them.

It's possible that a wall paradoxically increases fear, escalates the feeling
of not being safe. Once there is a wall, there is an Outside the Wall. The
other side of the wall grows ever more menacing in our minds when we
can no longer see it.

I've never gotten the walled estate I dreamed of when I read *We Have
Always Lived in the Castle*. But walls no longer look like safety to me.

Merricat Blackwood's fortress proved vulnerable, too. Ultimately, the villagers came. There was no way to keep them out—whether they brought
violence, or a pie and a conciliatory note.

At some point, the limits of physical controls become undeniable. The
longing for a wall is never truly satisfied by a wall. At the foundation,
and driving the placement of each brick, is fear. Mistrust. A yearning
for safety.

Fear is the thickest wall of all, and the hardest to knock down.

YOUR WALL, MY WALL

Among the abundant submissions we received for *The Walls Between Us* were essays that, at their crystallized cores, spoke with fervor, poetry, or raw wisdom to the multitudinous nature of walls.

We could not let these voices go.

And so, with the permission of the authors, we extracted those lines that spoke most directly to the themes of our book. We've paired those pieces, juxtaposed them, allowed them to create their own context and pluralities.

What is a wall?

A wall is this:

There were so many reasons to build fences: to keep the animals safe from the cars on the road, and to partition them from our neighbor's fields, and to sometimes have smaller areas for the heifers that hadn't been bred yet, and the growing steers who we didn't want to breed with our young heifers. We had special bulls for that, and we kept them in a separate pen. We built fences to keep a certain amount of sheep in one field, not to overburden the grass; one hundred in this field, one hundred in that one, and so on. Thirty-one thousand feet of fence line, just to enclose the perimeter of our property. There are fences that were built by my grandfather, rebuilt by my father and rebuilt again by my generation.

— LISA WITZ

I think of myself as a serial intimist. I crave
so much to have someone else in my veins.
I want someone else to know the poison of
living in this skin. But love and intimacy
aren't the same.

— KELLI LYCKË MARTIN

The thing is, I think we all walk around
trapped inside the invisible walls of ego.
I may be at the more extreme end of the
spectrum, but wherever we are, can't we
all allow life to crack us a little more open?
To become able to fearlessly reveal our real
selves to the world? I choose to continue on
this mission.

— SAUVIGNON SING

When the waves of depression recede, I get
to work. My task is to build an asylum before
the next storm. I am bound in mud. I scrape
up the sludge with both hands and slap it
into a small circle around me. With each
handful oozing through my fingers, I repeat
the mantra, "I am worthy. I am loved," in
the hopes that the walls of my refuge will be
built by these words. I must hurry to build
and give it time to dry through. I always
fail. The waves come. They wash away my
hut of muck, and I am left exposed, to strain
against the storm alone.

— DANICA LONGAIR

The red clay of these bricks spread before
me, unearthed long ago when this house
first became ours. Someone else built this
house of wood and brick. Someone who
raised their chickens in the yard that is
now my garden laid down these bricks.
Here. In a soil rich with leaves decaying for
decades, perhaps a century, I lay down the
bricks once again.

— CHRISTINE HUDAK

My life shifted that day in the hospital when I held my third son's motionless body, when I had to come home and sit on my sofa and tell my other two sons, just 5 and 7, that their baby brother did not come home—would never come home—from the hospital. To tell William he would not get to be the big brother he imagined. To tell Zach he would have no little buddy. That day they climbed over that wall with me.

— LISA SAMALONIS

Think of this market as the unseen circuitry igniting the flashpoint of child separation at the U.S.-Mexico border this past summer. This critical architectural coterie in the vast boundary enforcement apparatus—the scientists, the business leaders, the complex builders—makes public scandals like child separation both possible and tremendously profitable.

— GABRIEL SCHIVONE

It's all in the past now, but not forgotten: five endless years in a deadly camp in Northern Russia; my survival; coming to America; fulfillment of all my dreams and hopes; children; grandchildren... Life! My torturers? I forgave them. God won't.

— LAZAR TRUBMAN

I cannot stop the pig from being slaughtered. I cannot stop my father from marching on the street. I cannot stop my mother from taking us away from here. I can only watch my world get torn apart.

— ANNA KARPINSKI

For years I believed that the Berlin
Wall divided the whole of Germany,
snaking through the country's amoeba-
like shape, rising and falling over hills
and valleys, dividing fields and forests
indiscriminately. This fascinated me.
What did it mean to live in a country with
a wall running through the middle of it?
What happened on the other side?

— AMY MORAIS

The green line dividing east and west
Beirut fractured families, businesses,
and local governments. Kidnappings,
bombings, and depraved grabs for
power pierced through protective
physical and psychological barriers.

— MARY SIMON

Somewhere in the stacks of concrete
was a tagged traffic sign I'd established
an intimate routine with. Its words had
greeted me with a comfortable cynicism
each day since I hauled my belongings into
my new, post-divorce nest—wiping clear
my story of what once was in pursuit of
everything new. I'd nod as I shuffled my
feet home from days of too much work, too
little food, just enough vodka to dull the
pain. *Do Not Enter Love*, the sign read. It's
dangerous there, babe, it reminded me.

— JESSICA BRAUER

The words the woman spoke spilled
through my mind latching tightly onto
other thoughts, to my brother, to my
father, to seeing tiny kittens, their soft,
fluffy fur, knotted and twisted under
the green paint and in finality seeing
them dead. I knew that even if I could
somehow speak about any of these
thoughts, I couldn't believe there would
be a word of comfort or explanation to
the questions that I could never ask.

— MERCEDES TURNER

Behind the house is a brook-fed pond
that I use to come to when I wanted to be
alone and think. There was a little wooden
bridge that was just out of view of the
big house at the far end of the pond. The
rushing stream underneath pacified my
fears and washed away the tears without
harshness or judgment. The sound was
like my own private symphony of angels.

— JENNIFER SHIELDS

I raise my arms to scrutinize my weak, aging, pale and uninteresting flesh. The perfidy of my generous laughter over other-people's racism shames me. I am utterly, wholly, forever guilty, as I cocoon myself in colorless privilege, wrapped behind a safe and comfortable wall of silence.

— VICKI AUSTIN

The hope for a different outcome would cause me to keep reaching out to him, keep giving him opportunities to engage me in a meaningful way. This would turn into a pattern in most of my relationships. A constant laying out of my heart, hoping someone would meet me at my place of need, only to be disappointed.

— BART WHITTINGTON

Upstairs, I was at home and in love with every small room and crowded corner of Noni's "house." Upstairs was where Noni let me eat too many root beer ice pops, where I learned to roll meatballs, crochet (sort of), and sing along with Mitch. Upstairs was where I was allowed sit on Noni's lap at the front window while she leaned out to gossip with the other old ladies in windows across the alley. I'd always run up the three flights, in a hurry to get upstairs, the safest, funnest place, the place where love overflowed.

— LISA ROMEO

Orphan is both noun and verb. Like me. I am an orphan, a child who lost both parents so early that the words Mommy and Daddy were yet to my lips. I also inhabit the verb, to orphan, my vigilant psyche practiced at orphaning others before I'm orphaned again.

— SARAH CONOVER

As I matured, women remained a problem
for me. I tended to idealize their otherness
as exciting and mysterious, which in
turn left me vulnerable, for which I
donned armor and became a self-fulfilling
prophesy. I made up my mind that women
are to be loved from afar—besides being
mysterious they are also dangerous.

— LANNY LARCINESE

If something happened, I planned to go
down fighting. At the door, I flipped on the
switch for the outside light and loaded a
magazine into my weapon. As I cautiously
opened the door, there was a pale yellow
light just bright enough to illuminate the
steps outside my trailer—nothing more.
I heard the faint hum of a heating and
cooling unit sounding as if it were on its
last life, but beyond that the stillness of the
night struck me as odd in this war ravaged
land. Not even the birds were chirping,
and it was as if even the enemy slept.

— TAMMY ORTUNG

We asked ourselves: "Who will own this city? And how will it ever be united or shared?" We heard stories about brawls over expropriated houses and over inches of space that surround the holy places and that end up with no solutions for anyone. And thought, "Who decides what areas are holy and for whom?"

— SAMIRA MEGHDESSIAN

There were plenty of *blancs* in town, Lebanese and French, along with a handful of Americans, but along with the growing Gabonese middle class, most westerners owned cars. In Gabon, a car not only provided respite from the heat and humidity, but for a *blanc*, insulated you from the effect of your difference.

— MICHELLE HARRIS

There are no walls holding any one of
us back. Just as the moon sways the
oceans back and forth on a daily basis, we
too need to go with the tide.

— DIANE ORZECH

CONTRIBUTORS

JILLIAN SULLIVAN lives in a small village on a high alpine plateau in New Zealand. Last year she received the NZ Society of Authors Beatson Fellowship to write essays about place. Her twelve published books include award-winning creative nonfiction, novels, short story collections, and poetry. She teaches writing in New Zealand, in Philadelphia for Rosemont College, and in Pennsylvania for the Highlights Foundation. Once the drummer in a woman's rock band, and now grandmother of eight, her passion is natural building. Her latest book is the memoir *A Way Home*, on building her strawbale home. www.jilliansullivan.co.nz

DANA SCHWARTZ is a writer living in New Hope, PA. A lifelong reader and lover of words, she received an MFA from Fairleigh Dickinson University in 2008. Since then she has published short stories and essays in literary journals and anthologies, as well as online. She was a proud cast member of the 2015 Lehigh Valley Listen to Your Mother performance, and was selected again for the final show in 2017. Currently, she is working on a memoir about grief and motherhood.

FABIA OLIVEIRA is a graduate of Lesley University's MFA program. She is a Brazilian-American writer who writes about navigating both of her inherited cultures. Her essays have appeared in *Sisters Born Sisters Found*, an anthology, *Rigorous*, and a journal by people of color, *Your Impossible Voice*. Her poetry has appeared in Lesley's literary magazine, *Common Thought*. Her work is forthcoming in *Post Road Magazine*, *Crab Orchard Review*, and *The Indian Review*. She lives with her two children in the Greater Boston area and hopes to have a collections of essays out in 2019.

JESSICA GILKISON writes creative nonfiction in Madison, WI, where she lives with her husband, their teenager, and a trio of rescue dogs. Her background is in law, social justice work, and graduate-level clinical education. Jessica's writing explores loss, grief, and the evolution of resilience. She is working on essays and a memoir about parenting at the intersection of adolescence, mental illness, and the LGBTQ community. Jessica posts about writing at fixintowrite.com/author/jessica/.

BETH ANDERSON writes from her newly empty nest in Olympia, WA. She is inspired by many family adventures in far away places. When the nest was full she had stories published in *The Saturday Evening Post* and *The Timberland Regional Library Anthology*. She even managed to place in The Top 25 New Writers for *Glimmer Train*. Beth is now finishing a novel inspired by a magical trip to Iceland.

SHERRY SHAHAN'S most recent novel *Skin and Bones* (A. Whitman & Co.) is a quirky love story set in an Editing Disorders' Unit of a hospital. Her short stories, articles, and essays have appeared in *L.A. Times*, *Oxford University Press*, *ZYZZYVA*, *Exposition Review*, *Backpacker*, *FamilyFun*, *Country Living*, and many others. She holds an MFA in Writing for Children and Young Adults from Vermont College of Fine Arts and teaches an ongoing writing course for UCLA Extension. Adventures have led her to ride in a dogsled during the Iditarod, hike a leech-infested rain forest in Australia, snorkel with penguins in the Galapagos, and play polo in Barbados. She lives on the Central Coast of California.

KRISTINA MORICONI is a poet and essayist whose work has appeared in a variety of literary journals and magazines including *Brevity*, *Superstition Review*, *Lumina*, *Crab Creek Review*, and *Literary Mama*, as well as many others. Her work has also appeared or has been selected as a finalist in *december*'s 2018 Curt Johnson Prose Award in Nonfiction, *terrain.org*'s 2017 Nonfiction Contest, *Cobalt Review*'s 2016 Earl Weaver Baseball Writing Prize, and *Creative Nonfiction*'s 2011 Themed Essay Contest. Moriconi earned her MFA from the Rainier Writing Workshop in Tacoma, WA. She lives in the Philadelphia area and teaches in the Creative Writing MFA Program at Rosemont College.

VICTORIA PUNCH spent her childhood in East Africa, and grew up finding her voice in diverse intercultural situations. She is interested in the interaction between different worlds and is convinced that words have power to transform and bring about change across all kinds of boundaries. Victoria works in Bristol (UK) as a writer, musician, and voice coach, specializing in working with people who encounter difficulties in communication, language, and speech. She has a Classics BA, a Linguistics PGDip, and is a keen newbie in practicing mindfulness. This is her first foray into memoir. She can be found on Twitter at @victoriapunch_

ANN MARIE MEEHAN is an award-winning, published short-story writer who lives near Valley Forge, PA. She obtained her degree in English from the University of Pennsylvania and is currently at work on a novel of historical fiction chronicling the fortunes and failings of an Irish-American family in 1960s Philadelphia. She's also the Director of Communications for Arch Street Press, a non-profit press in Bryn Mawr, PA. Ann Marie, her husband, John, and their dog, Jennie Roo, are avid travelers and adventure-seekers. Their travel resume includes Morocco, where Ann Marie found a sympathetic dromedary capable of carrying her across the desert.

KATHLEEN LANGSTROTH was born in Toronto. She has been published in *The Radvocate* where she was runner up for the So Say We All Literary Prize. Online, she can be found at *Cold Coffee Stand*, as a guest blogger at Submittable, *The Galway Review*, and *Pendora Magazine*. She has twice been short listed for the Fish Memoir Prize.

TYLER DUNNING grew up in southwestern Montana, having developed a feral curiosity and reflective personality at a young age. This mindset has led him around the world, to nearly all of the U.S. national parks, and to the darker recesses of his own creativity. He's dabbled in such occupations as professional wrestling, archaeology, social justice advocacy, and academia. At his core he is a writer. Find his work at tylerdunning.com

JAMES THOMPSON was born in Fresno, CA, and grew up in Indianapolis, IN. He earned a degree in aeronautical engineering from Purdue University and went into the Air Force for 23 years, working on the military space program. After retiring as a Lt Col, he worked for several firms in the Indianapolis area. He fully retired in 1999 and began writing seriously. He is a published author with six books in print under his pen name, M. L. Hollinger. He has also had some success with short stories in the science fiction genre, which is his favorite.

JENNIFER HOPPINS is a creative seeker and writer of memoir, stage plays, short stories, letters, and poems. Her current project, a play for children and adults with math anxiety, is in production and scheduled for a tour in North Carolina. Jennifer writes for pleasure and practice as a way to uplift and make meaningful connections between thought, feeling, and behavior. Lovingly wrapped in family life, she also homeschools her son with her husband. Her next writing project is like a curious but shy friend, just waiting for the listening moment. She holds an A.B. in English Literature from Guilford College.

CARRIE PEPPER grew up telling her mother that she wanted to be a NYC editor, preferably with a high-rise office overlooking the Hudson. After working in sales for three global educational publishing companies—and seeing the conditions in which some of their senior editors worked—she scratched that from her list. Carrie is the author of *Missing on Hill 700: How Losing a Brother in Vietnam Created a Family in America*, a memoir. She is a member of the American Society of Journalists & Authors and has articles in numerous publications. She is an educational consultant and keynote speaker.

TRACEY YOKAS creates stuff. When she isn't writing, she can be found playing with paint, glitter, and glue. Art fuels her passion for connection.

Tracey lives in Southern California with her family and aspires to share her truth so others will know they are not alone. Each time she takes a risk and shines a light on her family's struggle with mental illness, the myths, stigma, and ignorance around life with brain disorders lessens. Tracey holds a BS in Communications from Ohio University and a Master's Degree in Counseling Psychology from California Lutheran University. More about her at traceyyokas.com.

JENNIFER R. HUBBARD (www.jenniferhubbard.com) lives near Philadelphia. She has written *Loner in the Garret: A Writer's Companion* as well as young-adult novels. Her shorter works have appeared in *Creative Nonfiction, North American Review, Hunger Mountain,* and other journals. When not writing, she is often out hiking. She is on Twitter as @JennRHubbard.

ABOUT JUNCTURE WORKSHOPS

BETH KEPHART is the award-winning author of 22 books and the 2015/2016 recipient of the Beltran Family Award for Innovative Teaching and Mentoring at the University of Pennsylvania's Kelly Writers House. *Handling the Truth: On the Writing of Memoir* won the 2013 Books for a Better Life Award (Motivational Category) and was named a best writing book by *O Magazine, Poets & Writers,* and many others. *Tell the Truth. Make It Matter.,* a memoir workbook, has been adopted in classrooms nationwide.

Kephart's other books include such novels for young adults as the critically acclaimed *Wild Blues* (Simon & Schuster); *This Is the Story of You* (Chronicle Books), a Junior Library Guild Selection, a 2016 Bank Street winner, and a VOYA Top Ten selection; *One Thing Stolen* (Chronicle Books), a Parents' Choice Gold Medal Selection; *Going Over* (Chronicle Books), a 2014 Booklist Top Ten Historical Fiction for Youth; *Small Damages* (Philomel Books), the 2013 Carolyn W. Field Honor Book; and *Undercover* (Laura Geringer Books/HarperTeen), a five-star book named to numerous Best of the Year lists. Her novels for young adults have been translated into French, Dutch, Brazilian-Portuguese, German, Simplified Chinese, Spanish, and Complex Chinese.

Kephart is a National Book Award finalist (memoir) and a winner of the Speakeasy Poetry Prize. She was awarded grants from National Endowment for the Arts, Pew Fellowship in the Arts, Leeway Foundation, and Pennsylvania Council on the Arts.

Kephart chaired the 2001 National Book Awards Young People's Literature Jury, chaired a PEN First Nonfiction Book jury, judged a *Family Circle* essay contest, and has delivered keynotes and lectures about memoir across the country. She has written for publications ranging from *LitHub, Catapult, Brevity, The Millions, LARB, Ploughshares Blog, Ruminate Blog, Chicago Tribune,* and *New York Times* to *Wall Street Journal, Salon, Philadelphia Inquirer, Shelf Awareness,* and *Publishing Perspectives.* She has led numerous writing workshops in elementary, secondary, university, and community settings. She has twice been featured in large, monthslong installations at the Philadelphia International Airport, was featured on the WHYY-TV show, "The Articulate," and was the June 2016 keynote speaker at the Radnor High commencement ceremonies. She is a partner in Juncture Writing Workshops, delivering five-day memoir workshops in selected locales across the country and producing a monthly memoir newsletter.

WILLIAM SULIT is the co-founder of Juncture Workshops. He has collaborated with Beth on multiple book projects as an artist, photographer, and designer. He is an award-winning ceramicist with a master's degree in architecture from Yale University.

Beth and William's first picture book, *I Can Do That!* (with Alexander de Wit), is due out in Fall 2019 from Penny Candy. They are at work on a series of illustrated journals.

JUNC | TURE

WRITING WORKSHOPS

———

www.junctureworkshops.com